Fireworks & Aftermaths

Reflections - Emotions - Observations

By

Andrew F M Wilson

Andrew F M Wilson

Reflections - Emotions - Observations Trilogy

Fireworks & Aftermaths
Vol I

Jasami Publishing Ltd will donate 100% of the profits from this book to charity.

Acknowledgements

Fine Art Photographer

John McIntosh

Jasami Publishing, Ltd

Thank you for believing in me.

Dedication

For My Family

Table of Contents

Preface	10
30	11
A (Final?) Cut	13
A Game Without Winners	14
A Glass of Port	15
A Menagerie of Sorts	17
A Whispering of Poisons	18
Abyss	19
All Lies Must Die	21
An Overspill of Madness	22
Ashes In the Dark	25
Bewildered	26
Black Carapace	27
Bring the Thunderstorm	29
Burning House	30
Car Crash	31
Catalyst	33
Catalyst, Part II	34
Chameleon	35
Charge!	37
Closing Time	38
Come And Go	39
Conversations	40
Country Torn	42
Crunch™ Time	43
Crystalline	45
Dark Places	46
Dawn is Coming	47

Depth	49
Do I Go Inside?	50
Don't Set That Alarm!	51
Down, Down	52
Draw Frozen	53
Dreamer	54
Emptier Still	55
Evening Promises	56
Eyes	57
F.U.C	59
Family	60
Family II	62
Fireworks & Aftermaths	63
Flicker	67
Footprints - In The Sand	68
Forgiveness?	69
Give Me What U Got	71
Guilt	72
Have I Been Here Before?	73
Heretic	75
Hiding, Behind Corners	76
I Should have Picked You Up	78
I Would	79
If….	80
In Bed (With the Dead)	81
innocence Lost	82
Insufflate	83
Insufflate, Part II	85
Just Another A To Z	87

Let It Go	88
Left Behind	90
Little Nephew	92
Me And The Whale	93
Memoirs	95
Midday Tears	97
Midnight Tears	98
Missing	99
My Sacred Place	100
Neon Monsters	102
Neon V2.0	103
Not Ours To Keep	105
Only Human	107
Out of Warranty	109
Painted Face	110
Paper Wars	111
Penitence	112
Quicksand	114
Rabbits	116
Reasons to Bleed	117
Remember Me	118
Run	119
Scar Issue	120
School Boy Pranks	121
Silent Cobwebs	122
Snake Eyes	123
Souring of Dreams	124
Stranger	125
Terror Nation	126

The Dead Inside	128
The Haunting of Nightmares	129
The Sea	131
To Whom Belongs This Laughable Charade	133
TV Dinner	134
Unicorn	135
War Without End	137
What Will Become of Us?	138
Other Works by this Author	139

Preface

This first volume of Andrew Wilson's poetry is being published in the middle of the first global pandemic in a century.

Although these poems are a reflection of his personal life, the sensitivity, creativity, and artistic originality reveal the feelings common in humanity. The poetry will evoke a myriad of emotions and that is so important to each of us at this point in time, as they illustrate the resilience of human nature and that we will not only persevere and prevail, but flourish and prosper.

This poetry is evocative of the essence who we are and so we can be inspired as we read and enjoy the expressiveness and eloquence of his language.

Michèle Bernadette Smith
Jasami Publishing Ltd.
April 2020

30

So… here we are, just turned 30.
Life is just the same? I'm still me.
Still trying to find the damn instruction book.
Still tripping over my tongue, my laces… my words.

Only thing that's different now is the arguments.
They are no longer about things like bed time, report cards and girls
They are now about mortgages and direct debits and phone bills
Yet the effect is familiar, I have replaced childish wonder with adult concern.

Where did Time come from? I looked over my shoulder, watching,
Yet still it found me, sleeping. Tick went the clock. Oh hell!
What am I meant to do now? Birthday cards tell anecdotes
While all along I taste the same air, nothing really changed.

I spent so long worrying about the calendar that I forgot to look at now.
My vision has quickly changed, moving swiftly toward an impending 40
And I doubt that the change then will find me any more surprised than now.
I'll just sit in a dumb stupor, bent silently over old poems and photographs.

I am more concerned for those around me. If I'm 30, what are they?
White hair advances on my loved ones, like a stain on the carpet,
I try to stop it; try to ignore the deep meaning of their grey,
The fact I am not the first or the only one gives little comfort.

So… where are my slippers? Time to turn the old fire on, to sleep
And turn the damn music down. Call that music? What's that you're reading?
Whoa! I'm my father now! Frowning at the kids in the street. Where're their parents?

Jesus! Yesterday I was those kids, hiding from the oldies as they looked my way.

It has occurred to me recently, more and more that Time has a sense of humour.
You could even say that it's sadistic. Gives you one side of things, blink... blink...
Look, you're at the spectrum's opposite. Old man with frown, glaring
And he is, in fact, no different than little boy with confusion, just a little greyer....

Andy 20.05.04

A (Final?) Cut

I have a need, a growing urge,
To tear at my flesh and to feel the purge.
To see the calming red seep down my chest
To feel the relief knowing I have done my best.

New scars to cover the scars of old
New pain to cover the agonies that hold
I'm deep in the chaos that I claim in my name
Should it matter then that the mutilation goes on the same?

Am I right in choosing this action to take away my pain?
Well, no it seem as I have slipped down again.
Blunted knife covered in dirt and remnants of old blood
Show the last time I fell face down in my melancholic mud.

What if one day I strike too deep, too close to the bone?
What would be the result from everyone I have known?
Clothing and careful light can cover the worst of my disgrace
But who doesn't see the pain and truth visible on my face?

Am I alone in this action? Do others feel as I do?
Struggling souls with no solution except to pull the blade through.
Who can understand the euphoria that comes with the pain?
Perhaps there's the reason I'm back here again?

When I no longer see a solution to the howls that keep me awake
That's when I need the wounds and the rage that they take.
An open arm with its free flowing crimson red,
Is the antidote to my virus that would see me dead.

The pressure cooker of life is much more than I can take
Every day I build up more rage and I never, ever get a break
So it builds and it builds until I scream and eviscerate
Praying with every cut that I can stop before it's too late.

Andy 25.02.11

A Game Without Winners

I'm sick of the turmoil, I'm sick of the pain,
I'm sick of picking myself up just to go round again.
I'm sick of the talking, I'm sick of the blame
I'm sick of telling everyone that I'm still the same.

I'm tired of the worry and tired of the rut,
I'm tired of ending every sentence with "but",
I'm tired of the lies and I'm tired of pretending
I'm tired of talking my way out of ending.

You talk and I listen, but no one really speaks
You talk and don't listen and it goes on for weeks
You talk and want answers when I don't now what to think
You talk and I stand there as hope starts to sink.

I think and you wonder and no one knows the game
I think and you answer, making me take the blame
I think and you shiver as my eyes begin their reveal
I think and you nod, trying to convince me we'll heal.

A game where no one really knows the design
A game without rules, except yours and mine
A game without end; a game without winners
A game that ends in silence with one or two sinners.

Maybe one day we'll figure out what it's about
Maybe one day we'll overcome the fear and the doubt,
Maybe one day we'll find that for which we yearn
Maybe one day we'll actually be able to learn.

Until then...

We'll talk... and won't listen.

Andy 27.06.10

A Glass of Port

May I share with you a thought for just a moment?
My mind has exploded with vivid memories.
The cause: A single glass of port.
Variety: LBV, 1992 to be exact, the make is unimportant.
The flavour flows, the mind blows
And here I sit, sipping my second, and reflecting.

I looked at the label, in the barrel in 1992, bottled in1996.
1996, you say? Where was I then? What happened?
How different was my world, my view, my hopes, my
fears?
Looking back, I cannot claim to be the same person.
Is the bottle that held the wine back then the same as now?
And am I the same? The same clown, crying tears on a
different stage?

1996! My grandfather was alive, was well; was still distant
to me.
I worked in a job I believed was for life; was my life!!
I was alone back then, on my own, no significant other.
A 22yr old who still held to the belief that life was mine.
I was the endless teller of jokes, the unimportant
chameleon.
Hell! Pour me another glass of the '92. Let me tell you the
rest...

And now for a slice of brie, not just any brie, but blue and
mature!
So when was that made? Last week was it? Last month?
Nothing new there then, is there?
Glass of '92 with a slice of '07 brie versus '92 me with '07
me.
Which one has matured with age? Not me in any case.
The port retains its life, the cheese its flavour. Me? I'm
musty, too much air!

Yeah, I know. All this from a glass of port! What am I
thinking?
Just how different my life was when that liquid was
bottled,

1992 in oak casks, me in school, 1996 in bottle, me in work,
And the truth is the bottle has probably learned more than I.
The only thing I've leaned from today, even after all this rumination?
Is that I should shut the hell up and drink beer next time!!!!

Andy 19.04.07

A Menagerie of Sorts

Can I be a man, just a man? Will you let me?
I don't want to be a son, a father, a friend or a lover
I just want to be a man; I want to be one thing.
Can I be a man?

Is it too much that I ask, to be given one title?
Just the one little thing, and not a menagerie of sorts?
I am too many things; I am diluted far too much
Yet I cannot be that which I want: just a man.

Okay then! If I cannot be a man, how about a person?
Why must I be labelled so? Why must I be a circus?
I cannot stand before you a simple individual. One!
I must be the entire goddamn chorus, and never a word.

I am not a riddle to solve, an opera to sing
I am me, a man, a person; an individual.
You treat me like a game board with twenty pieces
I am the player, you bastard, not the played!

Don't strum me, don't pluck me!
I am I! I am not your goddamn putty,
Try to mould me into what you want
And you'll find thorns where you thought was clay!

So you see, I am not what was intended, I am not a toy
I can make my own decisions; I can evolve my own design
I can step out of your shadow and make of what I can
So just accept the fact, that I am a man!

Andy 14.05.00

Don't know what this is, I'm pissed at the moment!

A Whispering of Poisons

How lonely is the world without the thought of you?
Why do I cast my eye there?
My ruined soul corrupted; I reject your healing touch
Why do I invite despair?
And when tears cast frequent shadows over everything we have
I cannot bear to see your pained and bitter stare.

Evensong is tuneless, the sunset has no lustre
Silently, I invite you to cry.
The wine is without flavour as I cannot find tomorrow
Even I don't know why.
My eyes look for truths in promises I demand.
Slowly… slowly… slowly I begin to let us die.

Will you still be here if I climb up once again?
Or will this time truly be our end?
When time lowers its veil and all we have is gone
Could I take the agony of losing my one best friend?
As the black beast of self pity sharpens its claws upon my back
I wish… I wish… I wish I could just truly mend!

So if I lay down and die upon a psychosomatic act
Is that really who I am?
Haunted pasts conspire in a whispering of poisons
I cannot tell real from sham.
Slipping into nightmare, as demons hold me fast
Where are you? I need you! Tell me you still give a damn!

Andy 27.09.11

Once more… for Maggie.

Abyss

So what if.
I was wrong.
All this time.

To err; hubris?
What if I wasn't meant
To run?

I've felt the lure
All my life
Yet still. I ran.

I
Must
Run.

It looms always
The abyss
There. Always there.

That yawning chasm
The endless depths
Black upon black.

But.
What if I wasn't meant
To run?

What I've given!
Gods, what I've given
To escape the gravitational.

But.
What if I wasn't meant
To run?

Time to stop?
Time to go?
Time to dive deep?

The abyss. Long feared
Long dreaded; long desired.
Time to take…

The plunge?

What if I was was always
Meant
To fall?

What if…

Andy 03.08.16

All Lies Must Die

To stand and stare at muscle
To deprecate the myoglobin.
The sybaritic youth pouts
As aged wisdom refutes.

No more can we lift the one ton weight.
With our arms; with our minds
But what of the social terrors?
Those we admonished... With time.

A grimace as we faced
The onslaught of a weekend.
We grimace now as we did then. We stare
In restful moments caught in reflection held in perfected
memory.

Time.

It did its worst.
We do not understand now nor did we then.
Tick, tock;
From where did our strength come, to where does our
strength go?

Aesthetically morphed
Or chemically enhanced?
We choose our version of a lie
Only to ultimately stop... and why?

Because in time...

From now to then,
From youth to pension....

All lies must die.

Andy 25.02.15 (Finished)

An Overspill of Madness

In a room with two people, it's way too crowded.
The ghosts have all the seats.
I stand in my corner, trying to be heard.
Words don't come, but thoughts do.
They fill my head as they tear at my mind.

Miles apart in the same room we stand,
I cannot see you. I see only unknown some ones.
They stand in my way, a vice like grip on my soul.
Talking, endlessly talking. I try to look at you,
But where are you in this ghostly menagerie?

Are you real? Were you real?
I check my scars. Yeah, they're real.
So you did exist at some point!
Or perhaps you are but a fragment of fantasy,
Made manifest by my desires; an overspill of madness.

Where am I? In all this craziness where am I?
Somewhere, perhaps in this very room, I found myself lost.
Buried, as it were beneath pseudo-moments and nightmares,
I re-enact what you told me; turn history into tragedy
While all along another piece of me withers and falls unnoticed
to the floor.

So what is left of who I became?
My life in a cocktail mixer leaves me once more devoid of
substance.
Unable to see, to think, to wish, to dream, to believe.
I am played out, a whisper lost to the chasms of the abyss
On a downward spiral toward the end, wishing, endlessly
wishing...

That I could just...

Just...

Stop!

Andy 02.02.10

Ashes In The Dark

I awoke this morning from another long dark;
Spent the night dining on ashes.
Memories played their solemn tunes for hours,
And I sat there alone, silent; a captive audience.

Visions of what were played by the hour
I turned my head to glower at the clock.
It laughed in my face, refusing to move forward
My eyes closed, and yet the onslaught continued.

How did I ever get to this place?
Wishes cast freely came true somehow, some-when.
Yet if I got exactly what I wanted why am I crying now?
Ashes, they are all that remain of once-crystal vision.

People around me conspire daily; planning cruelty.
I approach with smile, unaware of the secret government
That makes rules in my name, extracts blood by the hour,
I spend hours pretending there are no wounds, yet fooling no
one.

As the sun sets and the darkness arrives, I sigh and prepare.
Another night clock watching, awaiting the arrival of demons.
I pull the covers over my head, cross fingers, and hope in vain,
That this night will be different, and free from ashes in the dark.

I spent so long building fences, keeping out the night dwellers,
Realising too late that we weren't outside, they were already in.
The cry of night gives way to the flutter of ghostly wings,
As they nestle on the edge of my bed and begin their vampirical
feast.

Andy 15.05.06

Bewildered (At The Crossroads)

Where were you when my walls fell?
With only sad stories of my own demise to tell?
When I sat alone, covered in towels trying to stop the bleed
Where were you with the help that I really did need?

Where was the advice, so freely given before?
When I had slipped, crashed and lay broken on the floor?
When I cried out loud, desperate for any one to hear,
Where were you when I was stupefied by fear?

When did you all leave, how did I end up alone?
Is my current position a tapestry that I alone have sewn?
Or am I but victim to the cruel tides of fate?
Bleeding alone, wondering why I left it so late?

I spend so much time sitting bewildered at the crossroads,
Have I stories to tell of being here? Yeah, I got loads!
Grass is greener, the future's bright, I believed in all those lies
And now they're just one more aspect of myself I despise!

Empty bottles lie around the rooms, removing thoughts
My life is entombed in unopened boxes, sold in little lots.
This one here is marriage; this other one is youth,
Tokens of my lost youth, summarised by one milk tooth

How did I become such a mess? When did I fall from guaranteed grace?
Into this? A lonely drunken, broken fool, unsure of his place!
A once fruitful tree that's been stripped bare by insatiable greed
All because life has just far too many mouths to feed!

So! Where were you when my walls fell?
Would you like to hear more stories about my recent trip to hell?
And when I sit alone, covered in towels again trying not to bleed
How many diners will I be expected to feed?

Andy 06.03.08

Black Carapace

I need to go inside
Hide!
It's all gone black
Go back!
This isn't me.

I got old
I've been told
Cold?
That's my disgrace
I know my place!

Retreat!

Black carapace
End of race
I tried
We cried.
Shutdown

None of it was real
What I feel
Still the same
Blame game.
Erase?

Black carapace
Keep face
Stone cold
No hold?
Silence.

Wounds licked
End of conflict
No more to deem
Obscene.
Get up!

No more hurt
In its place

The black carapace
There never was a race
Left to win.

I'm...

Done.

Andy 26.05.19

Bring the Thunderstorm

He wrote and you replied. Words... Words.
I thought I understood. But the rage came.
You talked and I listened. But I did not hear...
Thump. Thump. My heart beat obscures your voice.

I create make-believe moments. They topple reality.
I am fiction in action devouring reason.
Taking truth and destroying. You look at me with sad eyes.
You ask why. I cannot answer.

I am idiot. I am demon.
I am the one to ruin everything.
Dark dreams and a fool's thoughts are mine alone.
A paradise reality and I bring the thunderstorm!

Do I tear open the fragile egg to check what's inside?
If so, I cannot put it together again. All the kings horses...
Grip it too tightly and it shatters of its own accord.
Too fine a grip and it falls, to shatter of its own accord.

I see the fear in your eyes that I have gift wrapped for you.
Seeds are planted, but what will grow, flowers or bracken?
Do I hold your hand and walk you down the familiar ruined road
of old?
Or do I have the strength, the courage, the belief to try
undiscovered paths?

Am I right to fear or wrong to doubt?
Should I stay where I am and roll my die?
Will you take this joy from me, rip me open and watch me
bleed?
Or should I thank you for the memory and run away again?

He wrote and you replied. Words... mere words.
I don't understand.
I talked and you listened. Neither can hear.
Thump. Thump. Heart beat obscures. Heart beat obscured.

Andy 12.01.10

Burning House

I saw the naked flame
That I reached out to touch.
I felt the warning signs
As I moved in even closer.

Sparks flew, drawn to the fuel
I was helpless as they touched,
One spark is all that it takes
To engulf what remains my world

Danger versus excitement,
Fear against hope, I wonder.
How could I avoid the flames?
They inch ever closer, immolation!

Do we dare to feed the fire?
Can we endure within or burn?
Truth is I want to find out,
I want to see, sleeping in the fire.

Where will we be, in the aftermath?
Warm; embraced? Or burned and alone?
Touch me; I want to feed the flames!
I cannot resist the temptation behind the fiery core!

Firemen warn me, take a step back.
Oblivious I run into the inferno.
What will happen when I re-emerge?
Burned, exhilarated, agonised or saved?

Only you can decide...

Andy 07.07.06

Car Crash

Did you see it today?
That horrific car crash?
Bodies strewn everywhere
People yelling, sirens wailing
The victims crying, asking why
Tears everywhere, mixed with the mess.
So I ask myself, what the fuck have I done?

I was the driver, you see; over the limit,
Speeding, reckless, unable to stay on the road.
I ploughed headfirst into a crowd of memories.
Places I've been, moments of tenderness, love,
All were thrown aside violently by my inability to brake.
Of should that read break? I don't know; concussion you see.
Where the hell are the paramedics? Can't you see I'm bleeding?

The rain started as I lay there unable to move, looking at my
victims.
Could someone stop that horrible screaming! Stop the
screaming!!!!!
The rain is washing the blood away, but I can still see it; can feel
it.
Will anyone here ever be whole again? So many people all
hurting!
Blinking lights and the noise of broken engines are all I know
now.
I have stopped the screaming. It was only me, only ever me.
But my victims are here none the less, just as wrecked as I am.

I lie motionless in my mental hospital bed while visions frown at
me.
What's that I've been given? I'm numb now, blocking out the
noise
Machines beep as I try to forget. For Christ's sake no visitors
please!
Someone has put a chair at each side of the bed. Who will come
first?
Will it be the ghost of Christmas past with her brown hair, her
eyes, her warm smile?

Or will it be the Promiser of Tomorrow, blonde, blue eyed, new
and dangerous?
Can someone call the nurse? Hit the panic button I need a third
alternative!

The police will come soon in the guise of my parents.
Or have I got that the wrong way round? I don't know.
The questions will start; I'll evade as usual.
To face my victims? I can't handle that, or the bitter pain of
choice.
How many of my friends will wear the look of The Stranger?
More pain!
I'll swallow past a dry throat as I weakly churn out my
supposition.
While faces leer and others cry, some will laugh as I weakly
beg...

Forgive me; I know not what I do!

Andy 01.09.07

Catalyst

You are my catalyst, my spark.
Without you I cannot ignite the fundamental fire of my life.
I exist now only in chameleonic form.
Every part of my being transforms at your merest whim.
A pause as I consider your emotions,
Another pause as I consider the part best suited to your needs.
I dance for you then, a miasmic metaphor of a man,
A windblown scarecrow, billowing in the face of your
chronological desire.
While in secret I wipe away a bitter, angst-ridden tear,
The one droplet of emotion that I permit my true self.

Will it always be thus?
Am I inherently bound to slavery without name?
A lifetime existing as mere façade?
Have I really fallen so?
I become little more than a facet upon which others may inflict
their wanton cruelty
Flick! Your desire changes.
No more do you require an instrument of sexual prowess.
Now I must be the punching bag
Upon which you lash out and lament your sequential failures.
I take the fall for you so that you may remain clean.

My price? I no longer have a heart.
It has transformed into a sewer drain down which pours more
than just my dreams.
Flush! And I am gone.
A once clean slate upon which anything could have been written.
Discard me and my ameliorative hope and then off to pastures
new.
While all along the people of my past continue their idealistic,
Yet futile search of my wreckage.
Ever hopeful that something of me may yet be found.
Though in truth, all that remains of Me is one discarded droplet
which once brought curses from my "Soaked To The Skin"
mother.

Andy 13.07.09

Catalyst, Part II

Back I go… Onward… Downward.
Through roads of self denial,
Through junctions of despair,
Into moments of idiotic self imposed loathing.
Will I enter the door you hold open with beatific flaunt and
sophomoric smile?
Will I cross the threshold of nightmares,
In order to welcome your minute moment of tenacious
tenderness?
Should I prostitute my soul just to make you feel better?

What a fool I am! What a bitter, resenting foolish man I have
become!
Sex is my master.
Dreams of male dominated superiority force me down the road
you demand.
And for what?
To restore the spark of youth you so desperately crave!
The idealistic view of yourself that only you seem able to see!
No matter that I fall then, victim of that which I abhor!
The Alpha Male, dominant in his desire to control the dance
floor.

The Dance Floor, a place I gave up long ago. A place so routed
in my self loathing,
That no manner of bathing can ever remove the psychosomatic
stench.
You go, honestly. Leave me here on the pavement. Enjoy your
predisposed freedom
In that place that takes you to that unobtainable altar of eternal
youth.
Remove the truth and replace it with myth.
Why not though? I've given my life to that endless, useless
pursuit.
I hope you enjoy it. I truly do,
As I walk away, unable to walk back down that all too familiar
road to self ruin!

Andy 10.08.09 (Finished)

Andrew F M Wilson

Chameleon

I am torn between what I have and what I had.
Too difficult a choice too easy to go mad.
I see shadows outside my vision, they speak
Giving false images of what it is I truly seek.
I can't trust them, nor can I trust my own mind,
So I tear at my eyes so the vision will go blind.

I can't speak to my ghosts; you see we've had a fall out
It happened so long ago, I can't remember what about.
There appears to be no one who will hear my point of view
But if the situation were reversed, I wouldn't listen to you,
You see I've made so many choices, not all of them good
And my life unfolds in a way it never should.

I yearn only to find the nexus point; the one bad seed.
I would pull it away, to watch myself bleed.
I can assume what's wrong, can harbour a guess
Pull it away, and then stare at the mess.
What happens when the bad is what's keeping me alive?
What would happen if I were, to hide, to keep, and to deprive?

People say I am changing, moving away from what is me,
But it was never, ever who I was, can you even see?
I played like a puppet pulled by so many strings
And now that they're cut, I find the wound now painfully stings.
I am not now what was. I have changed, I have grown and I have
fell
Nothing remains of what was me; there is no more to sell.

Who I was will forever remain lost; a mystery to tell
A story of the boy, who climbed, got stuck and then fell.
Reminders of old lie round every corner, I cannot look
Yet everywhere I see what was, I see the life you all took.
Am I a man? Was I a person? A guy? Someone you knew?
Only time will be able to tell which part of it was true

So I lock myself away, unable to face the probing stare
I stick a sign on my door "Madman here, beware!"
For I find it easier to consider that I am quite insane,
That way I am not forced to consider and point to blame.

I played so many parts, depending on where I was, what was required
Only now I can't find which part to play, so I slip down, afraid, cold and tired.

Andy 28.02.99

Charge!

So it has happened then.
The ropes have fallen.
The strings now cut.
So now I must face it
Alone.

You've done it again I see.
Stepped back from me,
Thrust me into the limelight
"Go to it, it's your show!"
You say, with water from your eyes.

No more pain!, you cry
Am I the pain?
A dagger in your side?
And must it be this way.
The two generals ready for battle.

Can't you see I'm tired?
Tired of being a `General'
No more battles I ask.
Please mother, no more battles.
No more wars, father, no more wars.

Andy 22.05.93

Closing Time (At The Twenty Four Hour Bar)

It's a quiet night. Not much happening.
The only sound comes from my sighs.
Little light from outside.
From out of nowhere an almost barman comes.
Excuse me sir, would you like some twist with your fate?

An imaginary glass sits nearly before me.
And I can help myself to the complimenting peanuts.
Ghostly memories of long gone companions brush by.
They do not see me sitting in the dark, watching.
Excuse me sir, did u enjoy the entrée of irony?

Did I hear my name being called? Or was it cursed?
Can't tell the difference these days, just glad I'm remembered.
Who put the juke box on? Oh, right. I did.
Stick a coin in my skull, I play the oldies.
Excuse me sir, tonight its free doubles on the guilt.

Yeah, go on; fill that phantom glass with phantom drink.
Let me have the phantom numbness.
Take away the world for just this next round.
Who'd like to join me? Raise your glass, a toast to nothing!
Excuse me sir, are you ready for your serving of remorse?

Time, gentlemen please. Finish off your drinks!
Funny that, I thought the drink was finishing me.
Is this glass imaginary, a memory or a desperate desire?
Well, there goes that almost barman. Shutters are down.
Excuse me sir, reception called, your anger has arrived.

Turned out into an imaginary street; the door gets locked.
I trip over an imaginary broken curb, I utter a curse.
Someone should fix that, I believe! Bloody dangerous!
Yeah, I know, but I haven't the time, and I don't know how.
Excuse me sir, I believe you dropped your comprehension!

Yeah, I did, a long time ago.
Goodnight, see you tomorrow.

Andy 30.11.06

Come And Go

People come and go, but they never really leave.
They visit in memory and that I really believe.
I have so many visitors at all hours of the day,
The keep coming and all have things to say.

How many people come through our every day lives?
How many lovers, friends, husbands, wives?
We close our eyes and we see childhood friends of old
Who are perhaps no longer there, to love and to hold.

Why do we lose contact with those we once held dear?
We see them fading, only to one day suddenly reappear.
Faded photographs give small clues as to how they might look
today
And when we see them we are at a loss, and end up stuck on
what to say.

Why do we always leave behind those that we love the most?
Their memories haunt our dreams like the rattle of a ghost.
What has changed? Why do we no longer feel that special
connection?
But suddenly the moment is gone, and all we have left is
reflection.

I have seen friends that I loved, would die for, and need so dear
Fade away from view and before I realise, they've been gone a
whole year
I make us swear that we won't leave it so long next time,
And when we repeat, I end up wondering, was the blame mine?

People come and go, but they never really leave,
In the end, perhaps that's not true, but I never meant to deceive.
Everything and everyone changes as we each move along
We're different people now, all singing a different song.

Andy 16.08.05

Conversations

I'm tired. Very tired. Do you mind if I sit here a while?
I'll be quiet, I promise. Let's face it being loud is not my style.
I've just come in from outside, and to be honest, it looks like rain
And I don't think I want to be caught out once again.
How does it know when it's time? When I'm outside,
Wearing just this tee shirt and jeans and not a single place to hide!

So anyway, how are you? Are things well and good today?
What's that? Sorry? You don't have anything to say?
Have you fallen out with everything? Oh, right. Just with me,
I understand; I don't know what to say? I guess it just has to be.
Do you want me to move on? Will I go back out the door?
Want me to go back to where it began? Back to where I was before?

I don't know how to tell you this, but I haven't the strength to return,
You see I used up all the energy, all the zest I had, in this pitiful run.
I just had to get away, the mirror was there, and the cobwebs were back,
They were all laughing at me, just laughing and I felt about to crack.
That's why I'm here, and why I apologise for interrupting your peace
But I thought you'd understand why, at least give me time to say my piece.

Yes, I know that I should smile, and that things can't be that bad,
But could you honestly say you'd be ok with the hassles I've had?
No! You don't understand, you think it's all just crap in my head,
Well let me tell you, you'd feel different if it was you here instead!
What I've given just to get here! And what's still left for them to take.
For God's sake can't you shut up? Just back off and give me a break!

Yes, I think that too! It *was* a mistake for me to come here I'll just go.
Don't worry, I won't bother you with this again, it's fine ok? No! No I'm fine, I just thought you of all people might perhaps understand
But what do I find? You're just like all the rest, withdrawing your hand.
Yeah, sure I've made mistakes and turned left when I should have gone right
But haven't you ever considered that sometimes the sun blocks your sight.

Just leave it will you? There's nothing more to say! You've said it all,
Even you! You of all people weren't there when I needed you, to stop my fall.
Well that's fine, just fine. I know when I've outstayed my welcome, uninvited guest,
I'm just another piece of shit under your shoe, one more thing for you to detest.
Yes, I know it's raining, so what? It's not like I haven't been there before, I'll dry!
So let's forget I was ever here, ok? Take care and good luck. So long, goodbye!

No. It's me who's sorry I shouldn't have come here. It wasn't right.
I just didn't want to go back there, not now, at this time of night.
Funny how the shadows change eh? The way they turn your attention in
The way they distort reality, make you believe you've no way to win.
Oh, wait a minute, I'm doing it again, am I not? Talking to the night.
What? Yeah, I know you did, and I guess perhaps you're right!

Andy 23.04.02

(A) Country Torn

Far away people in far away places
Avert far away eyes to make far away faces.
SI was but a stranger caught up in a strange land
Their customs and lives I could not possibly understand.
Armoured men stand by their armoured tanks
Is this the kind of protection for which they give thanks?
A tear-filled prayer turned to The One Above
Begging and pleading to keep safe the ones they love.

I walked in that land the people call their own
Who rules? Who lives and to whom is it home?
The leaders so far away in another place
The need to rule drives them on in yet another race.
The victims within so used to a war without end
Have no fears, still room at home for a stranger to spend
To lie in the safety of a comfortable bed, a decent meal
While outside our own brothers do break in and steal.

A country broken into a million pieces, North and South
While terrorist governments spread lies by ear and by mouth,
And turn others against what they themselves have built
Place all of the burdens on them 'til they fall, victims of guilt.
Who do you think you are? You know not of pain
All you can see is greed to further your own selfish gain
You fight so long for a cause you do not recall or know
While under the ashes your country is rocked by another blow!

Let's put this foolishness long behind each other
Stop hating your neighbour, stop killing his brother
The young innocents you maim and take away with your guns
Don't deserve it, you know, let the fathers love their sons.
Don't leave them to rot in some prison cell
Waiting in silence for the ring of the church bell!
Instead of killing the man with a different belief
Take him on side, lift his burden, help his relief!

Andy 07.08.96

Crunch™ Time

In you come.
Vultures feeding on the dead.
My carcass, your latest meal.
Doesn't matter that I still breathe.

I am dying, of that there is no doubt.
No life left in the powers that be
My soul is in the hands of the debtors
My life hangs, un-sellable. No use. No use.

I try to fight the encroaching darkness
I lack the necessary strength. I'm done.
Others around me try the same.
Yet their eyes are dead. Lost. Lost.

It's not The Now I worry over.
But End-of-the-month.
When the swarm arrives, insatiable
Demanding more than flesh will allow.

Again I will sit in skeletal, wind rattled bones.
Shivering, praying for non-existent warmth
I hear the wolves howling, the death of another?
While I try to protect those that I love. Futile. Futile.

Why have I once more come to this?
Uninjured, yet dying still!
Another world in which I labour doomed.
Taken, destroyed, in the name of reasons I do not understand!

Give it a fancy name, a catchphrase to be remembered.
Crunch you say? Yeah, that'll catch on.
Crunch, crunch, crunch, eat away another piece.
Tell me, what will be left this time? Who will be left?

Credit
Credit
Credit
Crunch!

Andy 10.01.09

Crystalline

Again? White on the black
How did I fall; why are you back?

Draw aching fingers through the white stained residue
One look in the mirror
Which one are you?

Who inhales real air?
Who only thinks they are there?

So much to do so little time
There is enough; just not enough is mine.

Frog marched through the every-day
Dance, puppet, dance,
Doesn't matter if you have a thing to say
You missed it, boy! You had your chance!

A life lived through a television screen
Reality traded in for a scripted dream
Is ultimately a life that no one's seen.
Little words left for a final requiem

Draw aching fingers through the white stained residue
Oh come on! Is this really you?

Wide eyed staring as the hours flying by
Take another why the fuck not?
Missed the proper talk, by whose who can cry.
Ignore both mind and body, choosing instead to decay and
rot.

The truth and lies might live forever,
I however, cannot.

Andy 03.10.17

Dark Places

My options narrow
No room left
What is left takes me to dark places
Where? I dare not tell!

Sun kissed beaches, they do not heal.
Bourbon, beer, wine are but hollow pursuits
Orgasmic amplifications no longer satiate.
Tell me where to go?

I have tried. I dare you to say otherwise!
I have bore more disguises than many a man can claim.
Still I remain heretical, fanatical… apathetic.
And still no one truly knows my name.

My options narrow.
No room! No room!
The dark place looms.
The abyss… again the lure of the abyss!

My options narrow.
I see no more paths
Where is the sun, the Moon, where?
Take me from this place!

My options…
Narrow.

Andy 02.11.11

Dawn Is Coming

Dawn is coming and I don't have answers.
Tumultuous flesh that midnight did not repair lies wanting in
the dissipating dark.
I taste today and it is bitter.
Who am I to try?
Birdsong plays its requiem for ghosts who'll fall today.
Perhaps it plays for solemn choices I did not mean to make.

I turn in the darkness.
My body follows a few seconds later.
Freezing cold sweat completes my fever.
What crawls in this pre-dawn eerie mist? Things to tempt flesh
and ruin dreams.
Is that another wing-flutter I hear?
The reverberations will be long and they will be destructive.

And now... Daylight fails, night smothers.
Hours unsaid poison the air.
Miasmic oppression, the true cost of things we did say.
Eyes tell lies while mouths refute.
Cuddles?

What are they but confirmation that guilt begins as doubt.

Take a deep breath:

And now to bed once more to lie in wait for the dark with its
blinding ability to absolve the guilt and to lay the final 24 hour
judgement over all that we did while creating new threads to
catch and tear and to remove the reality from the make-shift
dream that we recreate all in the name of progress.

The child envies the adult while the adult yearns for the child.

Thus we are reborn into an image we spent so long craving only to bitterly refute in this, our midnight hour.

Time to....

Stop.

Andy 14.05.12 (Finished)

Depth

I remembered there was depth in you, that I could see.
You were dark then, much darker than me.
I wanted so much to see inside
And now I am left wondering what did you hide?

When last I looked, I thought I knew;
Thought I had a chance, too good to be true.
Now though hindsight I can a take a sad look
And see it's not you who's read like the book.

What have I done this lonely past year?
What have I done to rid me of the imminent fear?
That in another year's time I'll still be the same
Perhaps trapped in a mind that's then gone insane.

With the cards laid before me I take another chance
And hope that I have not yet danced my one final dance.
Some choices ahead, a few decisions to take
How will I know if my choice is the right one to make?

I will try my very best to forget what I feel
Yet your image haunts me... my memory it steals
I see you look to me each and every day
I think of you and there's so much I want to say.

I wonder what you'd say, if only you knew
I wonder what would happen; what you would do.
I'm told by some people to just "Go with the flow"
Yet it would involve the emotions I could just never show.

Forget! Forget what I feel, it's the only way,
Yet I have no doubt these feelings will forever stay.
I'll ignore my dreams and I'll ignore what I feel
As for the working friendship... well, at least that's real!

Andy 17.11.95

Do I Go Inside?

It's raining hard, a breath forms.
Is stolen in the heat of the cold.
Feet hesitate as skin asks why.

There are Cockroaches in the corner,
And spider webs out front.
I hear the evening wind howl.

Dust covers everything; there is rot upon the walls.
Stains upon a floor.
I smell the stench of decay.

Paint once pristine yellows in the choking air,
Ceiling threatens to fall.
I cannot see outside.

Rusted key in broken lock,
As the rain corrodes the steps.
Do I go inside?

Nothing remains, nothing awaits,
Yet still I chase the dream.
A sigh betrays its tasteless truth.

A broken man in a happy home?
Perhaps a happy man in a broken home?
My heart aches. I no longer can feel.

I remain, as always.
Held fast.
In the quicksand of my own design.

Andy 30.10.11

Don't Set That Alarm!

Don't press that button, don't worry about time
You're four years old, little granddaughter of mine
Enjoy this time of lie ins and play
Leave the stupid alarm for a far away day.

Don't get up too early, conform, or fully dress
Lie with the dog, and just cuddle and think less.
Eat what you want, dance, and sing far too loud
And just bask in the love of the living room crowd.

Watch the crazy shows where all the animals talk
Don't worry what happens to Jack after the beanstalk
There's plenty of time to question everything we say
You're only four years old, it's time for play!

Be the princess chasing the dragon in castle halls
Be the little terror writing "love you" upon gran's clean
walls
Run and hide, quick! And give your daddy a fright
Suddenly remember something important when it's time to
say goodnight.

This time is your time; it will never come back round
When you have all day for play and to snuggle safe and
sound.
I wish we could stay in your beautiful world of sweet
halcyon days
And ignore the stupid adults and their stupid adult ways!

So whatever you do, please heed my advice
Keep to your stories about three blind mice!
Let your days be filled with love and with sweet, sweet
charm,
What whatever you do, don't set that bloody alarm!!

Andy 18.01.20

For Sophia. Keep on believing x

Down, Down

Sometimes I feel the world has too many people
Too many people all with too much to say.
Sometimes I look closer, take time out to listen
And sometimes I realise they all say the same.

This world in which I live is no paradise or Eden.
It is a hateful world made up of money filled men
So many tied to chains they make, chains that must be
For the world of TV makes us buy and pay in blood.

So many walk with heads bowed, their own demons dragging.
They sit upon their shoulders and pull them down and they sigh
And work more to pay for that which they do not want.
How many more will taste the bitter fruit that looked so good!

I lie chained to a noose round my neck and I cannot breathe.
Voices come through that chain and I must act to them all.
Selling my soul by the hour I grow less and less, the chain is heavy
And I will fall to the ground, voices yelling, demanding more.

Am I different to those captive around me? Do they see?
Do they bear witness to the same futility I see? Am I alone?
Big men with pockets that bulge look through me, I am but a number
I walk away and rattle while their pockets burst with my fruits!

I am called too bitter a fool and told to pluck once more
Pluck from the voices that yell in my face. I feel giddy!
Down, down they take me ever closer to the penultimate voice.
While all along I dream my dream, and I don't want to talk anymore!

Andy 05.07.99

Dedicated to the Twentieth Century!

Draw Frozen

"No. No. It's fine"
My own personal rhetoric, forever forced from unconvincing
lips through gritted teeth and insincere smiles.
Far better to acquiesce then to face solemn silences and caustic
retorts
Or worse still, a life without you.
Could I handle the cut strings and the absence of apology?

So allow me to parade before a bitter silence that lasts an eon.
Draw frozen breath from a barren future, what can I do?
Nothing it seems except accept an unforgiving lie that refutes a
past.
Hoist the flags and declare ground that will not yield
until you tell me to.
And how do I face a bended knee that's prelude to ritualistic
suicide?

I won't be there then.
For the ostentatious tears that follow
As you cry for your fallen sire.
Black veil that precedes a story of a bitter, wasted fool.
Would that I could stand in the shadows to frown the frown of
the unforgiven.
Who would sing my song?

I am but a means to an end; a truth untold.
I permit you the unadulterated tale.
I would be the king who failed; the god unborn.
While you would stand there, in a moment of perfect grief.
Tell a tale to haunt the youth; a ghostly want that follows in the
dark.
Beware, little child!

You may yet become... Him!

Andy 12.06.15

Dreamer

Crap!
Isn't that what people say
When you mention dreams
Those people would rather kick you
Than lend a hand when you "Fall".

Must I abandon dreams?
In order to become "normal"?
Must I kill of what's inside
To be accepted by "normal" people?

Why? I can see many wonderful things
Feel wonderful things,
Become wonderful things
But, these are all "inside"
Must I narrow my vision to become "normal"

Dreams are what guide me
My source of life when no one is there.
Why must you take this away
Is it jealousy? are you afraid?
That I will become more, as you grow less?

So I dream and ask
"Is my day done?"
Or has it perhaps just begun?
Well? I ask!!!

Andy 22.04.93

Emptier Still

Another glass emptier and I'm emptier still.
Do I head to the kitchen for yet another refill?
The walk becomes a stagger and the anger will rise,
Until the mirror reflects the demon; the one I despise.

Clock watching now; how many beers can I down?
Where is the line between Happy and Clown?
I watch for you coming then utter a sigh,
Then try to start living and try not to die.

So the actor is required the one who pretends
"No I wasn't drinking alone, I was out with friends!"
Sideways eyes that stare with questions unsaid.
A quick trip to the toilet to check my eyes aren't red.

Why do I do it, why spend my week getting drunk?
Searching the cupboards for all kinds of junk.
Maybe one day I'll understand and get to walk away.
Until then... Well, I guess I'll drink to that day!

Andy 10.10.13

Evening Promises

I promise to love you more.
I promise to always be here.
I promise to try and work harder.
I promise to give up the beer.

When the sunlight fades and night appears
It brings with us all our worries and fears.
We burn candles and lights to keep the darkness out,
Before it brings the troubles and explains what they're about.

Why is it easier to promise things at night?
Is it because the sullen silence can easily block our sight?
I guess it's just something I'll never understand
The way we twist and turn; the feint; the subtle sleight of hand.

Then with the dawn comes the realisation, oh what have I done?
A blinding panic brought close, and then fades with the setting sun.
Our human nature cannot handle the bright morning stare
And so like scurrying insects, we retreat away from the glare.

I'm so sick of promising the world at night, then calling myself a liar,
The morning light is cold and robs me of my desire.
At night I lie and speak, filled with a desire to succeed,
But with the dawn I awaken and my resolve begins to recede.

I hate evening promises that flow easily from my tongue,
Because I am the only person who ultimately ends up stung.
I feel less and less like the once proud man
And more and more like a foolish and stupid sham.

I promise
I promise
I promise
I lied.

Andy 06.08.07

Eyes

She stands in the same place every day, alone.
Eyes straight forward, never looking left nor right,
For fear of finding in a stranger's eyes
One more thing about herself she'd rather not know.
So desperate to hide the secrets about herself
Yet in the hiding she reveals for all to see!

A few steps along stand a couple
Him so tall, she so short yet they stand level.
A look of love that the madness around cannot break
Their hands meet; lips smile, their eyes shine, they touch
They do not care what is revealed, nor do they see anything else
Eyes only for each other and damn the world!

Behind is an old woman of indeterminate age
Eyes that dart left; dart right, dart up, down, around!
A look of fear as she looks at the world
So beat up by life, by love, by... what?
Her hands grasp nervously; she never speaks
But instead looks at others, looks at me, sees... monsters?

As we pull from the station a man sits down
The prejudice of life tells me he's not right
He stares! He stares at me, at *only* me!
Why? Does he hate me? Does he like me? Does he know me?
As I look back annoyed at his attention his eyes grow wide.
Fear?
He disappears inside leaving only his shell and I can't see him
anymore!

In a place that teems with life why do we stand alone?
We are little universes in too much hurry to let any one in
I look to the world: It's wonder; It's joy; It's... pain?
I do not know my mind in all of this.

These people, should I know them? Should I smile? Frown?
But the moment of transition is past and we all go our own
ways.

Andy 22.09.99

*Dedicated to the daily train journey, a wealth of material for any
writer!*

F.U.C

Come try.
For her if you can.
I dare you!
I'll meet you!
Come try for her!

You can't.
Have her.
You can't!
I'll stop you.
I dare you!

I found love.
I found her first.
How dare you!
You can't have her!
Don't try for her!

Don't try for her!
I need her.
We need her.
Don't try for her!
Please?

There's a fight.
If you want it.
You won't win.
We won't let you.
Don't try for her!

Don't try!
Don't!
I won't!
You won't!
You can't!

Please?

Andy 16.06.15

Family

There are times when we live with sovereign joy,
Much more than we do in standard, everyday life.
These are the days when you look to the sky,
And cry out with blinding tears because you live!

Tomorrow is my birthday and already I feel its love.
It is not a time of worry over growing even older,
But of a time when those around me cry out to welcome
The fact that I am alive and here for another today.

Who cares what happens tomorrow? Who really cares?
We have lost the will to enjoy every "Today".
Take it as joy to face, rather than a problem
To be overcome by hiding in deep waters until it's gone.

Tomorrow is my birthday, and already I feel its effect.
Friends and loved ones gather from all over with smiles
Smiles that signify I am doing something right with my days.
I will feel its love, even when the event has passed to memory.

I thank you all for this ever-present generosity you give to me.
I wander through different paths, unsure of where to go tomorrow,
Yet still you come to me on my birthday with tokens of love,
To give to my loving right hand while it offends with the left.

I awake to the sound of Christmas songs, coming from downstairs.
We run down the worn stairs with love in our hearts to accept;
To welcome the presents left to us at the cost of your supper.
Yet we still forget the fact that you starved to give us our toys.

The family will join us for a New Year toast to welcome time
Into our very home, we hug, shake grasping hands in love.

I slip away from the happy singing to complete a promise:
That never will I forget the two* empty spaces at the dinner table:

* "Fur Mein Oma und Opa!"

Andy 10.05.94 (Amended 27.09.96)

Family II

There were times when I lived with a kind of joy,
It was much more than standard, present day life.
Those were the days when I looked to the sky,
And cried out with blinding tears because I was alive!

Tomorrow is my birthday yet no more can I feel love.
It is a time of worry over growing even older, becoming less
It is a time when those around me cry out, but do not welcome
The fact that I am alive and here for another today.

Who cares what happens tomorrow? These days it is me.
I have lost the will to enjoy every "Today".
And once I took it as joy to face, rather than a problem
To be overcome, so I hide in deep waters until it's gone.

Tomorrow is my birthday, and already I feel its effect.
Friends send messages from all over with hidden frowns.
Frowns that signify I am doing everything wrong with my days.
I will feel its effect, even when the event has passed to memory.

I thank you all for this ever-present generosity you once gave to
me.
I wander through different paths, unsure of where to go today.
No more do you come to me on my birthday with tokens of
love,
I look to my loving right hand as it offends with the left.

I awake to the hollow sound of Christmas songs, coming from
downstairs.
I fall down the stairs, worn with love, and meet the faces
staring.
They hand over the presents left to me at the cost of my self-
respect.
Yet I still forget the fact that you starved to give me my toys.

Andrew F M Wilson

The family will join you for a New Year toast to welcome time
Into your home, they come, they hug, shake grasping hands in
love.
I slip away from the happy singing, not really welcome any
more:
And you look silently to the three empty spaces at the dinner
table!

Andy 10.05.99

Fireworks & Aftermaths

Fuck me! Another aftermath!
I'm sitting here again. Stunned!
Caught up once more in quicksand of my own design
Yeah, again! Why the fuck can I never learn?

Well, that's not true. I can learn new ways to cock up.
I am able, with blinding ability, to wreck and cause havoc!
I bring devastation not only to myself but to everyone else
Until again I sit with ears ringing from my own badly designed bombs.

I never set out to do these incredible explosions!
I walk slowly, humming songs and planning cakes.
Then suddenly I trip, lose my balance, grab on and light the damn fuse.
I used to have ironic laughter on stand by, somewhere...
somewhere.

Better watch out. There's another firework display heading my way.
5pm, gonna be a huge one! Quite a turn out this time, kids, kids, and exes!
Families gather to watch the explosions, they ignore, rightfully so,
The half-time clown as he slips on the ice and lands with a mighty bang!

So yeah, the aftermath. What happens now? They're always different
Sometimes they bring laughs, other times tears, some times pain
But always they bring the guilt. Guilt wrapped in layers of drink.
Temporary anaesthetic, habit now! Bang, boom and I reach for the glass!

It's quiet in here, only the ringing in my ears and the thump, thump of my heart.
No wait, I can hear something else, oh it's just guilt arriving.
And I'm sure I can hear cheers from the departing crowd, "That was a big display!"
Oh nice, someone found my ironic laughter! Oh Ha Ha!

Time now to look for a clean up crew, someone to fix my mess.
This time is different though, most of them have resigned!
I'll need to advertise in the local papers, or local bars.
"Wanted: A stupid person with no prior knowledge of bomb
making!"

Andy 07.11.07

Flicker

It changed in the flicker of candle light,
A shift of emotions going the wrong way.
Why? What did I do? What did you do?
Silence blankets the room. We do not move.

A sigh in the darkness, things left unsaid.
We turn the opposite way, back to black.
My dreams come, briefly, evanescent, they go.
I hear you breath, I hear you think. I hear you wonder.

Back into that place we vowed not to go.
Black depths of veiled midnight suspicion,
Whispers of infidelity and of betrayal compress us
Reaping what we sowed, now we dine on fear.

Heatless morning comes; we shiver in our solitude,
Compulsory words only, we talk what we must
Then onto our day with remnants of pain still etched
We waste our time, we waste our life and for what? For what?

One hand reaches out toward the other. A thunder clap and we're
back
Into each other, insatiable, in awe, in love, in time…
We save ourselves for one more night, light the candle.
Tonight we'll lie as one, pressed together, drowning in love.

Why do we continue onwards through countless emotional
shifts?
Delirious one moment then onto anger and pain the next.
I fear we are ultimately linked to that flickering candle, burning
on and on…
On and on, until in the end the flame will go, just one more
whisper in the dark.

Andy 20.02.09

For Maggie. Maybe one day we'll learn!

Footprints - In The Sand

I dreamed of you last night. Again
You called out to me.
Immersed in your beauty, your danger I almost succumbed.
I yearn to sleep forever at your feet.
To fall, head first,
To feel the water lapping at my face.

What would people say as they looked into my unblinking eyes?
Wet hair blowing in the breeze; the sand on my face
Could all say more than I ever could.
Sunlight on eyes that no longer see, a fire has gone out.
A love "afar" that claimed more than one future.
Could anyone comprehend?

I leave no footprints in the sand.
Who would notice they are not there?
I dreamed of you again.
Why me?
You won't leave me alone? I look to your horizon
I dream, I shiver, and I remember that the dead taste no tears.

People walk in that place where I would slip.
Would they pause to lament the fall of a fool?
A solemn stare at the summit from where I loved?
Flowers in a watery grave make no recompense
My sand remains clean; no signs to mark a life
Immortality through pain just not through progeny.

Andy 09.08.10 (Finished)

Forgiveness?

I am writing now, in the hope that you can hear.
That these prayers do not fall upon a deaf ear.
The things I believe now come into conflict
And my very soul, my life now become derelict.

I don't know what to say, to you both,
I don't know of any way to strengthen my oath
That I make now to you both when I say
I won't forget what you taught, what you gave each and
every day.

My love for you, Oma, Opa is more than words can reveal
Yet only when I'm alone, scared, afraid can I really, truly
feel.
I don't know when next I'll get a chance to say what I
must
Because the paths I am forced to take now shroud me in
dust.

With tears in my eyes and screams out loud, I conceive
A way out of this where I can at last, leave
Leave this foolish self judgement and self hatred behind
If I were to go, to hide, would anyone really mind?

When I think of you and the way you tried
To heal us all, I think it's me who should've died
For the fact of the matter is you are both better people
than I
So please, understand that it's not for selfish reasons that
I now cry!

Would it that I could go back and change what I have
done,
I would be to you both a better grandson
But we all live with today and yesterday, sadly not
tomorrow

So now I must repent, regret and be alone with my sorrow!

I am sorry!

Andy 23.07.97

To Gran and Granda. You have both occupied my life and my mind for so very long, I hope that you forgive me. Because I certainly cannot!!!

Give Me What U Got

I look at my pile, then look to yours.
I got own-brand crap, you got exclusive.
When you smile, it's at the zeros on your bank slip
When I frown, it's at the shit stuck to my door.

Someone else looks to mine
They want what I have; jealous.
I laugh in their face, because it's pathetic,
I imagine that you laugh in mine.

I buy a pint, while you buy the brewery,
I buy the cotton, while you buy the silk
I smile more than you, why is that?
Maybe because I fake it more than you do!

So give me what you got, I want it!
I'm sick of being little; I want to buy a mountain!
I go out to work, I laugh when you call it work,
I hate what I've become, and I hate what I was!

I'm in a foul mood, the reason of which is money,
It occurred to me how money resembles water.
Too much and you drown, too little… well, you know.
Yesterday I almost drowned; today I desperately need a drink!

Why can't we all have an equal share?
Flood and drought, just the sign of our times.
I look at you, sailing peacefully atop the flood
While I sit on the shore, with nothing but a leaking bucket!

Andy 26.07.05

Guilt

Got a visitor again, in the dead of night.
Yeah, my old friend "Guilt!"
Unwelcome, it slipped into my head.
Stole from me my restful eight hours,
Kept me talking all night, kept me dying.

The really annoying thing? It never spoke!
Just stared, just made me speak, made me near-cry.
Then, when the chirp-chirp birds started and the sun arrived
It vanished without trace, not even a footprint or flutter of wings.
How did it get in? I made damn sure I locked that door!

Where does it come from? I was almost certain it had left me for good
Then, when a suggestion of a crack appears it's back once again
Back on form! Back with unrelenting finesse and stronger than ever!
Go annoy someone else! There has to be others with more need than I.
But no, I am chosen it seems; handpicked to be the one parasitised!

Like a limpet it sticks to the back of my skull
Its filaments intrude, feed upon my psyche
With poisonous venom it saps my strength, devours my will
I sigh, the only real response I can offer my blackened, bothersome Beast.
Why? Why did I? Why do I and why didn't I? They're
Questions... they are only questions?

Oh for a sponge to lap up my languid inaction!
For a crow bar to up heave my monstrous visitor
For strength to overcome and for strength of conviction
For a moment's peace, for a smile, forever!
I yearn only to see a world minus my sins, minus my frustrations...

And perhaps, if only.... minus my gilded guilt!

Andy 15.08.10

Andrew F M Wilson

Have I Been Here Before?

Back again, stuck in the same old shit
The fact it's the same road, doesn't help one bit.
The traffic lines up; the radio plays the same old crap
And I fail to see, that I'm stuck again going round the eternal
lap.

The road's the same with the oft-learned corners laid out ahead,
My comments and attempts are no different to what's already
been said.
The adrenalin rushes, my heart misses a beat,
Yet I'm forced to wonder: have I been down this street?

New words assail me; they slam me from my track,
I again begin to wonder just what the fuck I lack,
What forces me down this filthy back dirt road?
As my perfect vision breaks down and begins to erode.

I sit in sullen silence, new worries form on my brow,
Yet I remain the only person who could have caused the now
I am faced with the guilt that tomorrow will surely bring
And I remain unable to face its deadly sting.

I sit in perfect-now, with the outside locked safely away,
Yet why do I fall now and silently begin to pray,
That tomorrow will not cause the agony I envision?
Brought irresponsibly forward by my drunken decision.

What the fuck will I be able to discuss when I quietly arrive?
Will I be even conscious of the fact that I'm alive?
Will I mention the pain that I've brought with my drink?
Well tell me, honestly, what the fuck do you think?

How long will we spend looking self-consciously away?
Hours spent wondering just what we're meant to say.
Why the fuck am I writing what I've done so many times?
Am I reduced to typing the only thing that rhymes?

I guess I'm just embarrassed by what I've gone and said,
Hours spend wishing that I had slept instead.
When I sound the horn and you come down your stair

Fireworks & Aftermaths

Can someone truly offer me a tried and trusted prayer?

There are some who would consider me the ultimate, stupid fool,
The one who learned painfully, and then broke every rule.
I tried to be the different one; the one who loved their wife,
But ended up the fool who never appreciated the perfect life!

Andy 01.08.07

Heretic

A heretical idiot hung up on being low,
A mind once sharp now emotionally slow.
A fruitful tree painfully stripped bare.
No wonder then that people stop to stare
At the ruin who fell and lost it all,
Still rubbing his head because he couldn't see the fall.

A life thrown away in spite of what he saw
Made up new rules then broke the law.
Wouldn't listen to anyone, regardless of who spoke
Now homeless, loveless, ruined and broke.
Did he have a chance to stop what he'd sought?
Could he go back in time to before he was caught?

Will there be anything left at the end to save?
Or will it all just collapse and go to the grave?
Little enough time to save what's left
And what is has found that love is bereft.
People will laugh and people will talk
But will anyone pause and take stock?

Let me be a lesson to one and to all.
The climb might be exciting but be ready for the fall!
Be happy with what you have, think before you leap
Because once done, there's nothing you get to keep!
Take the chance if you choose but consider my fall,
Nothing or no one can prepare you for losing it all!

Andy 21.11.09 (Finished)

Death, once more, by a thousand cuts!

Hiding, Behind Corners

You're out there. I know it
Hiding... evading... laughing.

I'm searching the corners,

Wondering... emoting... waiting.

The perfect life, I want it.
Memories yet to be... places not seen.

Laughter of children, of bank managers.

I'm waiting... waiting... wanting

Give me my life, let me find it

Lurking... concealing... tempting
You know where it is, I know.

I can play too... wait... wait... wait.

I'll scan the spectrum.
Infra red... ultra violet... blues

I'll look under the stairs

I'll search behind the pages.

I'll look around the corners.

I'll wait.

There is no hiding place forever.

Wait... wait... wait.

I'm still here...

Wait... wait... want... wait...

Andy 29.05.06

I Should Have Picked You Up

I should have picked you up
As you lay there upon another floor.
I mistook the red in your eyes.
I thought you would go mad.
I should have climbed up and spoke first.
But your silence held me close.

And why won't my eyes cry
When the rest of me painfully does?
Do they just care less?
When heart strains and beats in time to the rage only I can hear
Attentions wander within.
Why won't my eyes cry?

You should have picked me up.
Did the blood put you off?
Why? I am just as red as you.
Your eyes cried
As they saw what I have become.
But you should have picked me up.

Promises are silent now. Fuel spent.
No wind to carry their song.
Surreptitious stares cast we try to catch a lie
They are all that remain; they alone bear witness
To unspoken words with hidden meaning.
We should have picked us up.

Andy 10.05.12

I Would

I would ask differently of you
If I could
I would not promise so much
If I could
I would remember we are only human
If I could

I would not demand we live in the past
If I could
I would not remain locked forever in that past
If I could
I would watch us age and demand that we don't
If I could

I would give you much more
If I could
I would take away all your pain
If I could
I would make you happy again
If I only could

I would show you instead of just talk
If I could
I would be the hero in your story
If I could
I would change where I'm headed
If I could

I would show you I'm trying hard
If I could
I would live forever in our new world
If I could
I could of had it all
If I would

Andy 03.02.20

If....

My mind darkens once more.
It flees from the happy
To shelter beneath dank dreams others would call nightmare.
In shadow I regret
And lick wounds made fresh again.

I cannot stomach the serene
And mackled ideals repel
Cover me in darkness
I abhor this sugary-sweet day.
Accuse me of tangent and deny my refute.
Who is the real anyway?

Perhaps I am stuck when I thought myself free
Maybe I yearned too much
Amid the altar of choice.
What if I were right and you were wrong?
What would happen then?

What
Would happen then?

Andy 23.02.15 (Finished)

In Bed (With The Dead)

How quickly things can all just turn around.
How quickly we lose things that can never be found.
How quickly we lose those people, on who we can depend,
How quickly we find an enemy, where once we had a friend.

We go to bed each night, sleeping with the dead,
They twist and turn and suddenly they're deep inside your head.
They whisper little truths, and mess with what you know,
And suddenly you're down, floored by the unseen blow.

What did I say? What made you turn your back?
I just spent last night trying to back track.
I replayed the days events, and kept out the dead
And Christ only knows what it was I said.

So, see ya! You insane, stupid, and no-longer-amusing clown.
I won't be there anymore to help you with that frown.
What was I thinking; you were never a true friend.
You could never be someone special on whom I could depend.

Blurry images, unfocused thoughts, I just filled in the blanks
And now with clarity, I see the finished product! No thanks!
I did it again, lived a life in dream and made up my own rule,
Until in the end, it came down, again to just being everybody's
fool!

I listened without judgement to the crap you wanted said!
Until I went to bed at night, unsure of who was dead.
Did you feel better, after you dumped your troubles on me?
I was left confused, unable to even see!

Andy

Innocence Lost

We hadn't known each other
For very long.
Yet the pain of your passing
Hurts.
I looked at you, and loved.

I still think of you
Tender. Loving. Full of joy
Is it any wonder? I ask
That tears cascade once more
Down a painful face, as I write these words.

Ever since that fateful day
I still scream internal torment
When I think of the joy you gave
To me, your friend, your grandson.
I miss you Oma, I miss you.

Will my hurt ever heal?
At present I can see no end.
As the tears and rain run through you
No sound is heard. You never complained.
My god! I looked at you, and still I love.

Andy 29.05.93

Dedicated in loving memory to my dear, dear Oma. The things I never got to say.... I'm sorry it took three years to write these words, there just wasn't the understanding before....

Insufflate

Dare I insufflate; to stare at the mirror as it delivers?
Into my Parenchyma the excess flows.
I burn as I climb, who dares wins.
An aphorism long misunderstood as I claim precedence. This
time.

Deliver me from monotony;
advance me toward utopian ideologies as everyone else
stagnates.
Heart beat increases as minutes become seconds.
I am aware!

For the remainder of the night.
Until the next call of the unicorn.
Its white flank and singular horn beckoning amid the liquid
confusion.
At last - clarity amid the darkness.
No one else understands.

"You're really quiet now!"
Give me a minute - I can fix that.
Intrepid moments in a toilet cubicle,
Dare I inhale loudly?
I'm back - I can talk all night!
What? You want to sleep! Now?

It's ok; I'll talk to my pillow. All night.
It can listen to me explain the universe
Until even it succumbs, limp, and falls into apathy
I lie alone with the ceiling for company.

Who are we?
Then the morning with its blinding light and unforgiving
demands.

Fireworks & Aftermaths

Tie the tie and fasten the button.
Smile. Nod. Agree. Accept.

All the while ignore the unicorn.
Don't look; don't give in.
Who will win? Empty pockets or empty dreams?
There's a moment not long considered.

Victim or victor?
I still can't decide amongst the myriad of truths conjured up by
a poisoned brain.
I give in! Tell me!
Someone?

Who won this night?

Andy 24.03.15

Insufflate, Part II

I control
You don't
I'm not chasing you.
I decide.
I want... to...
Control.

I want control.
I hear you
I feel you.
Leave me alone!
I won't chase you.
You make it so hard not to.

I feel you
In my blood.
I feel you.
I feel the difference
Between a chemical heartbeat
And a heart... beat.

Can I stop
Chasing you?
I need to stop
Chasing you.
I can't
Chase you.

Cat scratches on painful skin.
Cough, sniff, cough.
Can't sleep, mouth's too dry.
I'm not moving. I refuse.
Doesn't matter if feet dance
And you promise.

I'm not going to chase you.
I'm not
Chasing you
I'll never chase you.
So you see?
I won this night?

Andy 03.10.15

Just Another A To Z

Another day, so here I am, me...
Because of pains I never tried.
Cry inside, as I begin anew.
Decision made and so it begins.
Every attempt brings more pain
For reasons I can never understand.
Go you say, with tears inbound.
Hard to ignore; harder to see
I cannot try again.
Justified though you feel, there is still the truth.
Kill it if you can; if we dare.
Leave it alone instead. Let it rot!
Maybe it's for the best
No chance of life in this desert.
Only dusty skeletons mute and immobile, held fast in decisions.
Perhaps they've the right idea.
Quantify the reasons with more imbedded half truths.
Read between the lines and consider
Suddenly options alter... Possibilities
Time then to recant? Perhaps not.
Until next time then... I will wait
Vicious are the ticks between the tocks, reminding us of the
ravages of time.
Who am I now?
Xenophobic, I hide; that's ok for now, here in the dark. But what
becomes of me in the mid day sun?
Yellow light that burns, that binds.
Zenith: I await your judgemental light

Andy 17.08.14

Let It Go

Let it go.
Can you?
Ancient history should be read, not felt.
You are out, and now you are in.

So what?

Live with it
It's not like it's the same *bored* game.

So can you?
Let it go?

I want to. I need to. I would die to.
Die to...

Let it all go.
Cathartic. Omnipresent.
Just a few words to describe it.

It.

A fruitless pursuit; a meander through the memories
A snapshot of the sybaritic, or an agony of the "ago"

It's all words, just words, and what are memories if not
paragraphs of paradigms?

I am after all, just a sum of my synaptic parts; nothing more,
nothing less.

So let it go.
Can you?

I will. I can. I have let it
Go.

I have let it go.

Cut up, rip up, delete, forget, and paint over.
Easy. It's that easy?

Isn't it?

Andy 15.01.11

Left Behind

When did I get left behind?
When did I lose touch?
I can see lips moving
I can hear people making sounds

What I don't hear is anything making sense!

There's Brexit and You-Tubers
There's voguing and Influencers with millions
There's being pansexual and asexual
And some people are self partnered.

There's gay marriage
And heterosexual partnerships
Couples are decoupling
And showing it all with insta-Book Face-Twits.

There's too much nudity
And not enough breast feeding
Television shows parade naked people dating
While people complain about swearing.

They say there're too many old white men on tv
And not enough young black people
Too many comedy shows, too much politics
And no way to tell which is which.

Big brother, love island
And goggle-boxing people talking television nonsense
People live their whole lives on mobile phones
And meet partners by the hour, swiping left or right!

Global warming leaves us cold,
And viruses named after beer
Mean no bread or toilet roll and holidays are cancelled
While presidents are fighting over who can be more dumb.

Teens talk strangely, eating data instead of meals
Have they had some consonants removed?
YOLO, and PM's; RT's and BRB; ASL and LOL!

And can someone tell me what happened to punctuation?

I don't understand!
Why was I left behind?
Maybe I fell. Was pushed, or missed one too many acronym!
As they say: SMH IDKWTD

Andy 10.02.20

Little Nephew

Welcome to the world little nephew.
I'm sorry for all the mess.
You see us men thought we knew it all
And that the world needed fixing.
So we invented the atom bomb.
And we taught ourselves how to use it.

If I had my way, little nephew,
You would not see such things.
People would smile and say what they mean.
And more importantly would mean what they say.
And smiling strangers would not induce a filial fear in parental
eyes.
They would just be friends you haven't met yet.

Don't get me wrong, little nephew.
There are joys and wonders abound.
Our ancestors spent millennia sculpting this place; some for the
good, a lot for the worse.
But there is plenty of time for that.
You need to find out who and what you are before you conquer
the world.

I can't wait to meet you, little nephew.
A few days ago you weren't even here
Now you are your own little universe.
A confused, fleshy blob all eyes and questions,
So I'll try to do my best and answer what I can.

I know what you will think, little nephew,
That I should know it all by now.
With the years I have lived I should be wise.
Can you imagine the lives I've lived?
But the truth is I'm not much more than you.
Still a fleshy little blob with too many questions.

Andy 29.04.12

Me And The Whale

Let me tell you about the two sides of my life.
On the left we have me, trying to make sense of things
On the right I have my whale, trying to eat the world.
We remain locked in mortal combat, battling to the end.

It wasn't always this way, once there was only little me,
Trying hard to be liked, to tell jokes, to tell the lies that made
friends
Somewhere along the line I stopped for too long with the door
unlocked
Then, without me noticing, I picked up this huge guzzling hitch-
hiker!

Now most of my days are spent looking at my expanding waste
line
And no, that's not a spelling mistake! If it's not a waste when
that is it?
In goes the gallon of ice cream, ohh, look! A new cheeseburger,
burp! Ahh!!
While all along I scream for him to stop, for Christ's sake at
least eat only one!

With a curse and resolution I throw another pair of trousers in
the bin,
Must have shrunk, I tell my other half as she looks down to the
whale,
Who am I kidding when I swiftly suck in my belly when I see
someone I know
The answer is no one, because now when I suck air this huge
hump moves onto my back.

Buttons strain, the belt is pushing back, angry red lines appear to
prove who's winning
Out of breath on that small hill, children race by so quick, I'm
overtaken by granny.
I need to sit down, need to catch a huge breath, fill my killer,
blue lungs to capacity
So that I can reach my door. Soaked with perspiration, heart
thumping, fingers shaking

Enough! Get the hell out of my body you huge, gigantic calorie guzzling monster!

Leave me alone, I want to be me again, get me trousers from the human rack,

Not from Freaks R Us, waist size three miles? We may have one pair, sir!

Just once I want to pick the clothes, not let the quadruple, elastic XXXXXL pick me!

I know, I know. There is no whale; it's just me and my gigantic mouth.

Eyes widen at the cakes, slam shut at the salad bar. Yup, dodged another lettuce!

Give me the T-Bone, go large, add butter, add lard, add salt, add cream, add heart scare!

Add another pair of trousers to the bin. Tell me, anyone a giant harpoon?

Andy 18.06.05

Memoirs

Time alone to think can be a dangerous thing.
It gives you the moment in which to ponder;
In which to look at what is happening.
And sometimes the realisation can be fatal.

When it is all broken down.
When all the irrelevant parts are removed
That is when we get a look at the polished product.
And that is when all else fades into unimportance.

To see the icy shadow of death creep inside.
To look into the eye of a loved one in the clutches.
What else seems important? What else really matters?
Petty concerns and ideas no longer have the same importance.

What am I trying to say with these words?
Am I looking for an easy solution to the problem?
Am I trying to get myself off the hook by looking?
I don't know; I guess I just hurt like hell!

To see another go the same path as one before.
I can't face up to the fears and grief that lie in wait.
I can't find within myself the strength I see in others.
At the end of it I'm like the little Kid who's lost his way!

Now months have passed since the fateful news.
Not just a virus, a cold, something curable.
The terrible ironies that taunt me every day come back!
And so now I face up to losing another close to me.

Close to me? Is that really a true, accurate perception?
Through my own selfish reasons he has drifted away
Caused by the anger I lashed out at the death of his wife.

Now as my Opa slips away, only now do I finally see the repercussions!

Andy 22.09.96

Dedicated in loving memory to my dear Grandfather, who sadly was taken from us on 27th September 1996. Gone but never forgotten!

Midday Tears

Scatter my ashes by my favourite sea.
Must I be dead first?
Most of me is already there.
The ebbing tide takes more of my soul.
I am pelagic. I don't want to come back.

This night the rain watched as I fell.
The Stranger stood amid the tears.
So long since I climbed; so soon since my fall.
Discarded droplets fill a mother's ocean
While the wind steals away her curses.

Ashes of a past no one can comprehend
Stain the beach.
Beneath the murky depth lies a man,
Devoid of substance, devoid of life.
Little fragments of regret carried upon the wave.

Is the wind just the wind?
Or does it belie a million cries of what should have been?
Wailing moments of inaction brought back to haunt.
Who speaks now?
My mistake. It was just the wind...

So I beg you, scatter my ashes by my favourite sea.
Those blackened remnants of all I was,
Who I am and who I wanted are so far removed from each other.
Was I even possible?
Discard my droplets; let another climb to these heavens.

Andy 08.09.12

20 years of pouring my thoughts out. Here I am... here I remain.

Midnight Tears

This night I watched the rain fall.
Falling like the midnight tears
Of some far stranger, cold and alone.
As the rain fell, so to did I.

The rain, I thought, was me.
Climbing a ladder to the heavens, then a fall.
Discarded droplets bringing curses
From a "Soaked to the skin" mother.

I look to the tear filled skies
And think of the others, climbing
What of those who have not yet reached the ladder
And what of those still waiting, still waiting to fall?

My rain falls not as water,
But as pity for those I pass in the streets
Walking with a "Gold for eyes" stare and
I think "how long? How long?"
'Til they join the skies, and rain.

Andy 08.09.92

Missing

Will I ever be able to find
That one small piece of mind...

That's missing?

When I add up all of my parts
And minus out the false starts.

What's missing?

It seems that my entire day
Revolves around running away

From what's missing.

I've poured another drink
Perhaps that one won't let me think

On what's missing.

Numb the pain; I can't ever feel
Unless someone could reveal

Does it matter? I'll drink like before
Until at I crash and hit that floor!

What's missing?
What's missing?

Andy 05.11.15

My Sacred Place

I drove the familiar road into my familiar sanctuary.
Opening the windows I was assailed by a peculiar odour.
It was not the smell of old; of the sea and of happier times.
It was the smell of decay; of things lost and forgotten.
I cried that day as I saw what my place had become.

Signs on the buildings bow in submission to the rust.
Weather and a lack of love have forced them to stoop so.
Net curtains in windows that once were proud; once said
"Come in!"
Now hang precariously under a heavy load of dust and neglect.
Where has the love gone? What has become of my sacred
place?

The sea is dull and cold now; it no longer sparkles in the warmth
of morning
Boats no longer rise and fall to the distinct sounds of tidal
music.
They lie beached, discarded and covered now with dirt and
abandon
The lapping tide gives out a stern warning now "Don't come any
closer!"
Even the sounds of laughing children are gone, lost in the eerie
silence.

Even the few remaining once happy places no longer give off
that smile
They reek of burdens, of forcing themselves to be there.
It's as though the very town is infected with a terminal illness
A few new buildings have ventured, yet they lack original
warmth
What or who has taken the life away? What have they done to
my sacred place?

I will return next year, no doubt of that. I miss you, old friend.
You who was there for me when my soul was broken apart
I'll not forget you, I promise. I'll even bring new paint if that will
help.
You are too dear to me to be discarded like an empty tin, you
saved me once.
So I'll think of you often in my dreams, you, me sweet and
sacred place!

Andy 09.08.05

To the town of Morecambe, my refuge in times of the soul.

Neon Monsters

As I leave the house
I am immediately
Attacked by neon monsters
Casting their products at me.

I try to run, quickly away
But there are more round the corner.
The one on the left screams "listen to me!"
And the one on the right screams "No me!"

Afraid to face more
I run into the house
And read the newspaper, more there!
Instead I turn on the TV, and still more!

Nowhere left to run.
Everywhere the neons cry
In a futile attempt I close my eyes.
Yet from the radio and airwaves they scream.

These monsters crave only our money
War ravaged people do not interest these beings.
Why should they. They cannot pay so why bother?
Looking closely it's easy to believe they're sentient

Us! The public, the consumer.
The brainwashed, the dumb.
We see their cravings, We hear their cries.
Yet strangely we see. The public still buys!

Andy 24.08.93

Neon V2.0

What now? What is it you want me to buy?
Something else I don't want, but something I NEED to try!
Do I own my own home? Is there something you can take?
Peel away all that I am, convince me it's all for my sake!

I press the button and immediately you scream
Coming at me from the sanctity of my own TV screen,
Flash goes the small print, the shit you pray I won't read,
While all the time you pester me, forcing forward my need.

Let's all laugh at him, the idiot who refused to listen to your ad,
He's the smart one, still the owner of all that he once had.
While here sits Mrs Jones, who wrote, who begged to sell
And sits silently with nothing, looking forward to a pacifying
hell!

Who do you owe your sins to? Who writes your small print;
your policy?
Who is left to face the cost, and who remains broke, who listens
to your say?
And when I press the mute key to wipe away the sorcery, you
attack by post,
Barely awake I approach the mat to listen instead to your
appointed ghost.

Is there nowhere I can go without you trying to empty my bank
account?
Must you tempt me with "My unique Rate", a special, private
discount?
I open up my wallet, give you access to my cash-card and pay
cheque,
While you tell the shareholders, and forget to mention whose
you made wreck!

I am but an army of one who turns off the TV; who shreds the
mail you send,
But wake again to face your assault and look at the concern you
pretend,
Audition the actors who bring the look you need, the look of
empathy you can use

So you can sit in ivory towers, the sports car outside and the ability to choose!

Andy 21.10.03

Not Ours To Keep

I sit now and think of all that has been and gone.
Of all that once stood with me as important.
Funny the way these priorities change.
Hilarious, the way we can laugh at yesterday.

What upset and bothered you yesterday?
What stood out in your mind, taking you from sleep?
Can you look at it today, in the warmth of day
And honestly laugh at the silliness of it all?

Of course there are times when yesterday's annoyances
Become tomorrow's fatalistic worries.
Life threatens us with change each and every day,
And we must learn not to fear it at all!

Matters of love stood up to haunt me yesterday.
A whole day of life spend worrying, crying, fearing.
only to be replaced today with renewed vigour!
And all concerns melted with the promise of more.

In order to save all we love and cherish
We must be prepared to sacrifice it.
Because the more the hold it, the more we need it
The easier it becomes to lose that which is not ours to keep!

Andy 13.10.97

Dedicated to all those who can understand.

Only Human

Sometimes I can make a mistake.
Sometimes I can even lose direction
And I have been known to just fall down.
But what, I ask, can I do?
I am only human!

Is it human nature to err?
Is it written on our heads
On the moment of conception?
Are we born intent on making mistakes?
We are, after all, only human.

Do you, like me, sit and wonder?
Do you sit in quiet times and contemplate?
Are there times when you feel you can't see tomorrow?
Do you feel that today has served only as a lesson in sadness?
It can be justified: You are only human.

It's funny, don't you think?
The way we can look at something good one day,
Then look again another and it's just not the same?
Isn't it funny how the very angles of life are changing?
Is this what it means to be human?

The hourglass of time can wear itself thin
Just like the past mornings we all have done.
The visions of our past go with us always
Sometimes blocking out the light of today.
I guess it's only human.

What point am I trying to make right now?
I really don't know... or care.
The burning desires of passion are strong
And hold me fast this fateful day

But then again, it's only human.

Only human!
An excuse made so long ago; used by so many.
The eras of Time hold many an excuse.
They hold us all deep in their fashion, and wait.
But I guess that's only human...

Andy 13.03.96

Out of Warranty

Excuse me!

May I see you please about these knees, as they seem a bit done
And this shoulder I bought on sale seems quite frail
Can I exchange it for another one?
I now realise I've a problem with these eyes, they used to see much more
And I wouldn't normally mind but these ankles do grind
And make quite a noise as they walk on the floor.

And I must explain about this brain that used to be so fast
As for this hair! Well, I'm beginning to despair
Because I don't really think it's going to last!
And I've got his belly that wobbles like jelly; it didn't do that before
See these hairs that sprout, what's that all about?
And how the hell do I turn off this snore?

What's that you say? Out of warranty! That's not good advice!
I've spent so little time in this old body of mine
I expect some features to work more than twice!
It's not my fault that my legs called a halt and some teeth need filling
How can this be, you saying this is all down to me
I've still a long way to go, you know. god willing!

So!

For better or worse in this final verse I guess all that's left to say
Is that beauty comes from within, so be proud of your skin
Because we're all - everyone of us...

Out of warranty!

Andy 13.03.20

Dedicated to those who don't take life too seriously. You're my kind of people!

Painted Face

Is it that time already?
I'm late for my public appearance.
Time to put on the make-up.
Is it straight? Covering the scars.

A painted face, is that all there is left?
Pretty colours to hide the black heart
That lurks beneath even the warmest smile.
It signifies the truth that none can see.

Lastly, the plastic smile.
I place it on carefully, obscuring the tears
That lie in wait for the moment of weakness,
That lets out its torments in waves of grief.

I am so tired of playing the friend,
To those who need to hear the whispering tones
Of one who understands. Yet I'm not expected to fear
the time when reality seeks me out!

Where were you then?
Do I no longer matter to you?
I pledged myself to hear and comfort you,
Yet when it's my turn you turn away without concern.

Hear me now! In my moment of reckoning,
I weep bloodshed tears for those I've left behind
While I try to heal myself, yet you do not understand
The wretchedness behind the plastic smile.

The painted face! A sad reminder
Of a brutal past, carved in tears
From those who love the actor behind the acted.
The true carers of a face without paint...

Andy 18.01.94

Paper Wars

Rows and rows of people, all gasping for air
A racial filled glance, a vengeful dirty stare.
From around their little camps they play their war
Never asking, never caring for what they fight for.

Lines of division set between you and me,
Build the walls higher, until we're unable to see
See past the gun turrets and empty coffee cups
Just curse and shout back as the fury erupts.

You don't care who I am, or what I do
To tell you the truth I couldn't care less about you.
You hovel in camps at this morning's daily brief
Fuel the fire on the hollow foolish belief.

So many different camps, all blurting out defence
You've become so corrupt, you don't make any sense.
The paper is armed, the photocopier is loaded.
And there's an empty desk already exploded!

The victims lie around, crumpled up in bins
No one really understands, no one really wins.
At five-o clock it's over, the field lies silent,
No sign at all of the soldiers, foolish, fanatical, violent.

The office war itself is a very stupid thing
Started by no more than an innocent telephone ring.
I wish I could get out, walk away from this stupid war,
But the working day is what this bloody century's for!

Andy 03.03.99

Dedicated to the Monday blues, is there anyone who ain't had it?

Penitence

When I was a baby, so I'm told,
Not being able to recall such an early age,
You'd hold me in your arms and talk
And stare with pride at your new-born grandson.

When I was little, and just a boy, I'd sit, amazed
Watching as you'd create, for me, some masterpiece.
A small toy made from just the basics, but from the heart.
These were the gifts that no moneys could buy.

When I was a little older, a teenager.
I remember Friday nights filled with joy.
We'd sit together, you, me, Gran, warm even in winter
As we watched the television, and laughed at the cartoons.

I remember birthdays, Christmas, New years.
I remember the smile as we'd toast each other.
And how can I forget the firm shake of the hand?
The love and strength gripping mine?

Where did we lose it? When I was older,
 Nearing the end of teenage, we fell away.
The hand shake and pride-filled smile disappeared
And all that was left was duty and obligation.

Now that you are gone from us, I can grieve.
Can view painfully clear the broken links.
To this day I cannot wish in the new year, or Christmas
Without feeling the empty despair echoed in my parents' eyes.

All you wanted from me, towards the end
Was a single pint; a night with just the two us.
Grandfather and boy. Yet I denied you even this.
I have no answers why, I guess no one ever truly does.

There are so many things I need to say.
Yet you are not here, and to say them now be too easy.
Would take away the meaning they had in life,
And I guess all I can say now, today, yesterday is....

I am sorry, Granda.

Andy 02.05.97

Quicksand

How much is too much
When too little is the reward?
When fecundated demands
Holler louder than desire;
When hubris calls and no one understands
And I am left to explain.

Who will grant me absolution?

Blame me, then.
Because I explained between the lines.
When celebratory outputs pour forth
And weekend excesses are laid bare
Don't blame me for truths that not even you can stand.

Let me sit.
Let me sit here and seethe.
I promise it'll go away.
Tomorrow I will be the me demanded.
Today, I have fallen head first
Into the quicksand of my own design.

For now. Please. Let me succumb;

I'll be me again
When the music stops and drink is dry.
I'll be me again. Somehow.
I'll smile and make believe.
I need to seethe. Right now.
And abhor the hubris of those I have chosen to accept
Right now. Leave me be.

Tomorrow I'll be the Me.
Today? I simply cannot be anyone.

I just need to be no one.
I have tried for too long to be someone.
Just for today, please...
Let me be me one last time.

Before even I forget.

Andy 08.08.16

Rabbits

Where has all the magic gone?
Esoteric magicians with clandestine rabbits,
Amusing everyone and fooling no one.
Love was forever and hope sprung eternal.

Dreams? They lasted a lifetime and wishes cast freely were
listened to.
Was life really like that?
Of have I applied rose coloured paper to standard glass?
What a truly funny thought, lamenting a work of Grimm fiction.

Hours lost parading charred, smoke blackened memories to
unmoving crowds
Melancholic choices that were forged in iron while the
blacksmith did but laugh.
I hum a tune no one understands. They clap, just not in time.
While would-be conductors shake their heads in unison, berating
the improvised melee'.

What happens when wants become haunts?

Plastic faces with paint spattered eyes, there is no truth here.
Crumbling vision torn down by cruel retorts;
Refutes that cannot bear close scrutiny, I play them all.
While you sit there with cold clad stare. Blaming... shaming.

I am but a rabbit caught in the headlights, chasing carrots and
chasing tales.
Won't someone please tell me who I am?
Lie with me or lie to me, the difference is there between a
heartbeat and a sigh.
Choose your stone and throw. We'll sit together to watch the
ripples form in perfect silence.

Andy 30.12.10

Reasons To Bleed

There are just too many people and not enough air
Just feelings and highs, and the occasional despair.
Have I taken too much on, and have I lost my place?
There are just too many people, all yelling in my face.

You could argue that I should know where this would lead,
Yet even I was unprepared for the amount I'd have to bleed.
So many issues all jump up from behind
And I'm supposed to smile and pretend that I don't mind.

I stand here now, miles and miles away
Struggling to come up with the things I'm meant to say.
I read the latest headline, now I need a choice
I swallow past a dry throat and try to find my voice.

I can look deep into your eyes, and can I see the trust?
Yes, I can. But it's only because I must.
We've given so much, lost and gained so much
Now I find I'm committed, because I'm addicted to your touch.

Even when we sit alone, there are other people around.
They sit and wait in darkness, trying not to make a sound.
Turn on the light, to see them scurrying into the night
Sometimes I feel that it's they who should stay, and I should take
flight.

But like I said, I love you so much, and now I cannot leave,
Just tell myself you love me too, I try so hard to believe
That it's me who's won your heart, and this time it's for real
And hope I'll not end up a sad and lonely joke because of how I
feel.

Andy 23.03.08

Remember Me

And so as I stand now and silently stare back.
All I see now, are charred remains, burned and black.
A place I once thought, happily, as my second home
Now twists, contorts and becomes something so sadly unknown.

What can I say now that the time there has been and gone?
What can I do, but look ahead with pride and back with scorn,
For I offered to give you all my very best and to try so very hard.
But the memory of your betrayal cuts deep like a broken shard.

But there are still those who's memory I will fondly recall,
And there are those I will watch gladly as I see them take The Fall.
For those that I will miss, and sadly leave behind, I offer a prayer,
It's not all bad. Just look after yourselves and please... take care.

Remember me when I'm long gone and no longer there to blame
The times it's your lives that fall around you think back with a hint of shame
Over the way I fell because of your self righteous ideals and vice
Just remember, I stood out; I was noticed and for that I paid the price!

Remember me friends and colleagues, in times of need.
For those few I will always be there, to hear and to heed.
I promise to stand by as you have stood by me as the blame was dealt
Your loyalty; your concern and your compassion, as always, were greatly felt.

You all know who you are!!...

Andy 22.01.97

Dedicated in "loving" memory to my time and friends, both true and sarcastic, at PCL.

Run

Run, run, run all the time!
Run here, run there, run every bloody where!
That's all we seem to do as people, as mice, as cars.
We run to the shops, to the pub, to the bus.
We run from the work to the home, then back again.

Wouldn't it be nice if some giant hand
Were to reach out and stop the world.
Let us all stop, catch a breath and look.
Glance quickly at the halted world, and laugh
But laugh quickly, for we'd soon have to run again!

Andy 09.09.98

Scar Issue

Open the knife, then open the arm,
No one need know the reason I self-harm.
The blood pours out, the pain subsides,
No one need know where the reason resides.

Cover the wound and hide the shame,
Because no one else could understand this game.
Blot out the reasons, pretend I'm ok,
Because I don't have words, don't know what to say.

Years pass and I have only old scar tissue,
I have the knife on standby, awaiting the next issue.
Smile for the people, ignore what's underneath,
While in the left hand, pull the knife from its sheath.

Bang! Goes the pain, as the knife lands a blow,
I sigh with pleasure, because only I know.
Blood washes away the agony for a while,
And I can feel better; can even put on a fake smile.

Days spent covering the wounds, so one can tell,
They don't even know of my recent trip to hell.
As the red fades, to be replaced with the white,
My body is a mess, and I don't like the sight!

It's been years since I found myself in this place
Tearing flesh to my unimaginable disgrace.
Staring eyes glance along my ruined skin,
Do they wonder, I wonder, what goes on within?

Andy 18.05.06

Dedicated to those who know.

School Boy Pranks

Where does it come from? The sudden stinging slap,
That hits you in the face, feels like a thunder clap?
You walk a quiet road alone, with nothing going on,
Then suddenly you're humming loud, a new and different song.

My brain has turned peculiar, gone and flipped around,
Everything has a different beat, new words and new sound.
I don't know when this happened, or when I lost my brain.
The truth is hard to take, have I possibly gone insane?

Am I making sense to you? Cause I certainly ain't to me!
I have no sense of self, I have no way to see.
Swimming now in strange seas, with a different kind of wave,
My knees have turned to jelly, because I know I'm not that
brave,

My life has had a quiet coup that's taken out my sense,
I have no way to comprehend, or measure the recompense.
I feel I can't escape this force, that's headed fast my way,
I doubt that when it gets here, I'll even know what to say.

I have no way to understand just what is for the best,
No easy way to just sit down, and quietly take the test.
This life we have is all we have, the only one we'll get.
What point is there, of standing there, afraid of getting wet?

30 years spent hiding, afraid to meeting my fate.
I looked out past the walls, only to find I'm late.
All I want is a chance, and not wind up kicked down,
To be able to be serious, yet still remain the clown.

Now I've gone and done it, and I feel such a fool,
For lowering my defences and losing my cool.
I played this game of life and death; I played it with my dreams
But with my school boy pranks and games, the truth is rarely
what it seems.

Andy 26.09.06

Silent Cobwebs

Today I awoke tiredly, a pain in my chest.
The ghostly sunrise, gives little light at best.
The mirror stares back, eyes of black, glare,
With the heat of the stranger, lurking there.

The wooden door creaks in the hall, like a voice,
A distant whisper that yells out its lonely choice.
The wooden stairs mumble and groan as slowly I walk,
Their lowly voices whispering at me in silent talk.

I walk wearily into the dust-filled forgotten hall.
The sunlight shines, highlighting the broken wall.
I try to look out the broken glass windows, of mine,
But I find, sadly that the vision has eroded with time.

The family living room I walk to, gives little back,
The glistening cobwebs are there, hiding in every crack.
I look fondly around for signs of an abandoned time,
And realise, that the sands really are short and fine.

I scream out loud for a chance to see remembered views,
Yet the choices I made stick to me like tight, old shoes.
Instead of the warmth and the remembered safety of my bed,
Lie empty discarded packing crates and a rusty new cobweb.

The vision of a forgotten past is my very host,
As I try once more to forget those forever ghost.
The light shines in, weakly and with a grudge,
And I slip once more into my life of sludge...

Andy 21.03.95

122

Snake Eyes

Time to throw the dice,
Examine the dots on the canvas.
Lift the chips, place now your bet.
Gamble your life on a whim.

Snake eyes! Take away my vision
Dealer smiles as the pit boss nods.
I fall to the borrowed chair, throw again?
Why the hell not? I've nothing else to lose.

Rip off more blood, can I have more chips?
I need to bet again, can I have the dice?
Here goes my soul, quick, catch the dice,
They've hit the floor before me.

Send me to the front door, beneath the glitzy lights.
They promise the world, while measuring your coffin.
All bets are off, nothing left to gamble,
Just wait for old Lucifer to call in his chit.

Pockets turned out, watch the moths fly off.
Like emotions on the wind they climb, fall.
I watch them go, ripped from my skin by dice.
Is that rain? Perfect, just perfect. I sold my umbrella.

The bank is closed. Nothing remains in the account.
Not even a smile opens the door, no free coffee.
Catch the look from the rich as they hold the door,
It's not open for the likes of me, move aside, fool!

Cardboard box for a palace, shopping trolley for a car.
Eat the roof for breakfast, when I want to eat the rich.
Neon snake eyes beckon from the horizon, like laser beams.
Never blinking, never caring, never remorseful. Always there.

Andy 26.09.06

Souring of Dreams

As I sit alone in paradise, I try to be content.
I think about the memories and all they represent.
I had assumed my hunger would leave, grow less by the hour
Yet now I face the facts as The Mighty Dream turns sour.

The gangs of teenage terrors lurk just outside my door
I have a garden, yet don't dare go there any more
You see I am afraid, a coward! Too scared to face my enemy
And instead create new fears of which there now are many.

Would you be content if you had all that I have, if you were me?
Would you fight the fear that grips your balls, the fear that I see?
Or would you cower inside to make new psychosomatic foes
That feed your fear, your terror, my very petty woes?

Who can I take this to? Who would understand? A shrink?
And if I did go, what would he really, really think?
"Grow up you fool, and take it all like a man!"
Yet in the end even that dear dream is nothing but sham!

I don't know what to do, as my terror wakes to feed
It takes more and more control, takes more of what I need
I don't know how long I have until I really end up mad
And who would really notice if one more dream wound up bad?

Andy 06.04.00

So it's still here after all!

Stranger

I look in the mirror
And it's not me I see.
In place of my eyes
Two dark pools look back
Full of forgotten ghosts
Crying for remembrance.

The boyish face I knew so well
Doesn't stare back,
Instead a man's face,
Full of the worries of the morning
Looks back, annoyed at being disturbed
Who is the stranger looking through me?

Opening the curtains of the familiar room
I look out to see unknowns staring
Looking at the outside me
Wondering where I've gone
I'm still here, now
Looking through the world as a stranger.

Andy 12.10.92

Terror Nation

I was born today. Do you know that?
I came from the peaceful womb into the world
Today, my world is a country filled with grief,
For my birth was met with bombs, with death, with pain.

People died today. People just like me, walking, running,
driving.
They went to work in order to pay their bills and buy their gifts.
They had their breakfast, they kissed goodbye, and they went on.
Until the bang that silenced even the most innocent decided to
come.

Debris that once was cars, once was streets once was… people
litter now
They lie silent, denied even the chance to cry out at the faceless
cowards.
The streets have run red with blood, we weep, we cry, we
wonder,
We do not understand. What is it you hate so much? How can
you hate so much?

This vile hatred must stem from somewhere. Is it our ideals?
freedoms? Our lives?
You look at us and plot, you bring fear, acid words and now,
today, you bring bombs
Bang! Out went the light that was so many lives, are you proud?
Pleased? Happy?
What do these lives signify? The black smoke rises from the
ruins that were people!

I am ashamed to be born into the world of Man. I hate what we
have become.
We are race of faceless killers, religion-bound by hate to destroy
all that is different.
Do you even comprehend the word tolerance? What is it that you
are afraid of?
Yesterday I had a world that was secure; today I will eat
terrorism for my supper.

So what I am I meant to feel now? Should I *tolerate* you?
Understand your ways?
Long have I tried to give up any hate that I had, yet now you
force feed me.
My Television screen feeds me images of death; it fills my belly
with anger!
I wish I could kill you! Yet only yesterday, I couldn't
comprehend even killing a fly!

So here I am, on this day, admitting to all that I could easily kill
a human!
And in doing so, I must force myself to admit that you are
human; are as me.
Yet never before, even in my darkest dreams could I envision
death from my hands.
I hate you. I hate what you have made me become and I hate
what you still plan to do

Andy 07.07.05

*Dedicated to my fellow humans; the innocent lives that were
taken from us in London today.*

The Dead Inside

Pull at my eyes,
Make me turn my head.
Something within me dies
But why am I smiling instead?
Murdered thoughts rise from the dead
Dismembered feelings come alive
I utter words that I've already said
Why, if I've climbed am I now about to dive?

The dead inside begin to move
Zombied remains hungry for blood
What do my remnants have to prove
That would turn polish into mud?
Does the herd of cattle consider the cud
As it consumes without reason?
A painful emotion that swells to flood
In the face of another descent into treason.

In the end, who would remember
The face of another broken clown
Left with little else but disiecta membra
To explain the onset of frown.
When the truths are faced and gloves are down.
Who could claim they would not fail
Hollow promises have very little sound
When the wronged, suddenly see and begin to wail.

Why then do I turn those eyes?
Why then do I die inside?
Once again am I the one I despise?
When my inner world can no longer hide?
When all is gone what use is pride?
Nothing new in this sad moue of an idea
Just wreckage from a two-world collide
Handed down to those I hold most dear.

Andy 01.11.14

The Haunting of Nightmares

Now I'm digging deeper this hole I fell into
And narrowing the sides so there's nowhere to run to
The ground rises higher away from my grasp
And the ceiling I lowering, I let out a gasp.

The rising panic engulfs my very soul
It's tearing it out, swallowing me whole.
I cannot speak for fear, nor can I even see
The little remnants that are all that's left of me.

The stability of old has left me these days
And leaves me now in a bleary kind of haze.
I cannot see past the chains on my chest
And all I can manage is a little smile at best.

Faces so scarred leer from behind their broken shell
As I try to convince myself that all is still well
Fear not, I say. A little hug will take it all away
My unspoken fear: Will you still be here today?

Your icicle tears they do shatter on the floor
And the warm smile is gone, I can't see it anymore
I cannot find the strength to laugh, nor can I cry
Yet despite the failings of my part, I still blindly try.

Awaking from slumber to the rise of a new morn
Makes me realise how I've been, how deeply forlorn.
I curse at myself, realising the good things that are mine,
And with that thought in mind, I can again see the sunshine!

Andy 04.01.99

Andrew F M Wilson

The Sea

I am drowning.
Been treading water.
Can no longer stay afloat.

Ocean blackness below me
Stormy night sky above
Nowhere do I see shore.

My arms are shaking.
Legs refuse to move.
I taste salt water.

Lungs burn with every breath.
Shallow breath, too little air.
My mind begins to shut down.

I am cold. So cold.
Lips quiver in blue.
I cannot feel... cannot feel.

I see a rescue line thrown my way.
I cannot reach it. Will not reach it.
So I tread my water, waiting to drown.

Voices call from the distant shore.
I ignore the impassioned pleas.
I slip deeper. Gasping, water enters my lungs

She is near. The Siren and her song.
Haunting me, calling me, luring me.
She takes away the salt water. Almost...almost.

Shore appears in pre-dawn light. Far. Too far now.
I have not the energy or the desire to reach it.

I'm done. Drowning now in my own sea of creation.

Down... down.
Deeper, darker, colder.
There is no fear, no pain.

Just a feeling of regret... almost.

Andy 19.09.08

To Whom Belongs This Laughable Charade

When reason becomes treason who will care? The exile or
the one who was there?
And when emotions have fled and anger is last.
What becomes of a down and out iconoclast?

Bereft of the chance of immortality
Left instead with a million chances of hollow wordplay.
When instinct fights response who understands the
game?
The end is the same; there's always someone laying
blame.

To sit in the aftermath as little more than an afterthought.
How many would re-evaluate all that they had sought?
An expunged foetus is that all you can parade?
Whose life is the ultimate, and to whom belongs this
laughable charade?

A once tiny part that thinks itself the main
You expect me to sit here and claim the insane?
Caustic moods from little more than a teen
Thank the wonder of evolution that I possess a spleen.

For what else is there to listen as I vengefully vent
Pouring forth oaths against all that I hate and resent.
Tied up in knots as the lies consume what I have built.
Away goes the future to be replaced once more by guilt.

So I lock the door on life as I lock the bathroom door.
Tear away pieces of myself to cast them on the floor.
There's another mirror into which I cannot look
Remembering for just one second all of my life that
someone took.

Andy 19.11.15 (Finished)

TV Dinner (Do You Want War With That?)

I turned on the tv and what did I see?
A man pointing, saying me wants to kill me.
I don't understand; why does he want me dead?
It's not me or my family aiming a gun at his head.

Just because we're different and don't look the same,
Is that any reason to kill, hate and maim?
Underneath the clothes and different colour eyes
Is another human being; not some animal for you to despise!

The politicians tell lies; try to make us understand.
We're too busy nodding to see the sleight of hand,
As they whisper schemes and plan to divide the spoils of war,
We are the ones left wondering what it was all for.

Let's make a new super-villain; one to scare the people!
They bomb our homes, so we bomb their steeple.
We take their land so they blow up our commuters,
We see it every day, played neatly on sterile computers.

A nice little war to watch while we eat our meals,
It's easier this way, no one ever feels.
These people that die every day on our media's front page
Never get a chance to explain the reason for their rage.

We're all victims here, in a scenario without conclusion.
Just little puppy dogs force-fed a delusion.
We all need an enemy, so let's fight until the end,
Set out to kill a stranger, end up wounding a friend.

Who started this all? Where was I when it began?
Was it when the towers fell; when all those people ran?
Does anyone know what the hell we are fighting for?
In the end, isn't truth always the first victim of war?

Andy 28.03.06

inter arma enim silent leges

Unicorn

What have I got?
A wife, 2 cats, a huge house,
2 living rooms, 5 bedrooms, 2 bathrooms.
2 cars in the drive, 10 guitars adorn my walls.
Rows and rows of possessions, of things.
I have no debt; I have money in the bank.
Add it all together, and it equals a void.

A super-massive black hole surrounds me,
I suffocate in its unrelenting dark pressure.
I lie like a victim of a terrible car wreck,
Pinned under the wreckage that was my life,
I gasp for breath, I gasp for air. Help.
While the weight of the ocean towers above me.
I try to swim, yet gravity holds me to the floor.

Memories are what move me now.
Unable to breathe, to function, to think.
I recall the unicorn of my youth.
The lush fields filled with wonder, of waiting promises,
Barren now, desolately devoured by insatiable mouths.
Cobwebs fill the well now, dust covers everything.
Even the sun is gone, obscured by the smog.

What do I have?
I have a cage inside my chest.
In it, the prisoner of my youth berates, sits, ponders, atrophies.
He pounds the bars that were forged by my (in)actions.
I used to be that youth, now I am the jailer!
Grease drops from multiple chins, huge belly heaves, eating my life,
The bones of my desires are stripped, and then thrown to the hounds.

A jellied carcass is all that remains of my 6ft body,
My bones are long since crushed, skeletal structure ruined.
The weights of my life have taken my form, moulded me to this.
I am a cartoon caricature of that which I aspired.
A black and white slap-stick, there but to amuse.
The thumbscrews are tightened, my life squeezed once more.
And I no longer have even the tears to back up my cries!

Andy 22.12.06

Yeah, it's Christmas again! Bollocks.

War Without End

I used to see the world through your eyes.
Now all I see are places I fucking despise.
No one listened or heard my cries.
No one even bothered to say their goodbyes.

Tears falling at night, they make no sound,
Especially as there is no one around.
People couldn't handle the wreck that they found,
Couldn't handle seeing a friend who hit the ground.

I started this war and everyone took a side.
True pain and anger were unable to hide.
To hell with the hangers-on just there for the ride,
I've lost the most! My trust! My honour! My smile! My pride!

Innocents falling, they cause the most pain,
Because they will never, ever be whole again.
People look at me and ask if I'm insane.
They walk away, come back, and ask again.

War without seems to be my bitter fate
A life time of drinking and dining on self hate.
Was I the target or was I merely the bait?
Guess I'm just the idiot who found out too late.

Am I angry at the moment? You bet I am!
More and more my projections are mere fucking sham!
Show me a slaughter and I'll show you the lamb,
And here stands the one person you really should damn!

Andy 01.04.09

What Will Become of Us?

What will become
Of us
If love is not enough?

When words run dry
And kisses die
What will become

Of us?

Will I still matter still
At day's end?
Will you?

I fall again
With autumnal leaves
Fall. We fall

Again?

Colour drained and withered
Is this what I've become?
a barren tree littered with rotting fruit.

Bury me then.
In refuted pasts.
Bury me then.

I was never meant to last.

We could create a pseudo us.
A perfect replica of a perfect idea
Then and only then

Can the real be forgotten.

Andy 12.10.16

Other Works By This Author

Reflections - Emotions - Observations Trilogy

A Garden of Monsters Vol II

A Museum of Moments Vol III

Fireworks & Aftermaths

Printed in Poland
by Amazon Fulfillment
Poland Sp. z o.o., Wrocław